PANTHER
VS
T-34
Ukraine 1943

ROBERT FORCZYK

INTRODUCTION

We had nothing comparable.
Major-General F. W. Mellenthin, Chief of Staff of XLVIII Panzer Corps, referring to the T-34 tank

The German Wehrmacht invaded the Soviet Union in June 1941, confident that its superior doctrine, training, equipment, and leadership would carry it to a swift victory over the large but clumsy Red Army. In particular, the German panzer divisions, composed primarily of Pz III and Pz IV medium tanks, had proved to be powerful spearhead units in the Polish and French campaigns, and it was assumed that they could deal with any Soviet tanks. However, German intelligence had failed to detect that the Red Army was re-equipping with a whole new generation of weapons, including the T-34 and KV-1 tanks. Within the first weeks of the invasion, it quickly became apparent that the new Soviet tank models had superior firepower, mobility, and armor protection to that of the Pz III and Pz IV tanks. German panzer officers were shocked that an army that they had regarded as backward was equipped with tanks that could destroy any German tank, and they demanded a quick technological solution to match the T-34. Yet in many respects, the T-34 had not reached its full combat capability. Inadequate training and doctrine had marred the T-34's combat debut in 1941, and the Red Army spent most of 1941–42 trying to figure out how to best use their technical edge. It was not until the Stalingrad counteroffensive in November 1942 that the Red Army could use the T-34 to its full potential.

By mid-1943, the Red Army had perfected the T-34's early technical defects and had a cadre of trained tankers who knew how to use it properly in combat. However, the German technical solutions to the T-34 – first the heavy Tiger tank and then the medium Panther tank – would not be available in significant numbers in the summer of 1943. As the war in the East approached a decisive climax in mid-1943, both sides sought to achieve dominance in the realm of armored combat. The Soviet approach was based partly on numerical superiority but also on fielding a reliable, well-rounded tank. The German approach was to build smaller numbers of high-quality tanks that excelled in one or two areas, such as armored protection and gunnery. The stage for this decisive clash between two competing philosophies of armored warfare was set primarily in the Ukraine, which offered the best terrain for operational maneuver and which contained key economic resources that Germany needed for survival. If Germany could maintain its control over the Ukraine, there was a chance that the Red Army could be fought to a standstill. For the Soviets, victory in the Ukraine would establish the necessary preconditions for a successful drive westward into the Axis heartland. Ultimately, the battle for the Ukraine would determine the remaining course of World War II.

The actual combat effectiveness of each combatant's armor units was the sum of the quality of their tanks and crew training as well as tactical doctrine, battalion-level leadership, and logistic support. By 1943, the German advantages began slipping in part due to heavy German losses but also due to the Soviet ability to learn from defeat. With fewer tanks available than the Red Army and a diminishing cadre of veteran tankers, the Wehrmacht sought to gain superiority in tank warfare through technological advantage, such as the new Panther tank. The Panther was designed specifically to outclass the T-34 in firepower, mobility, and armored protection, and the Third Reich put enormous financial, labor, and industrial resources into developing and deploying the Panther for the decisive clash in the Ukraine. Hitler, in particular, had an almost religious faith that new weapons such as the Panther would turn back the tide in Germany's favor.

While the Germans focused on the technical potential of their new tank designs, the Red Army doggedly developed their T-34 into a no-nonsense weapon with great operational potential. Possession of the reliable T-34 in large numbers would enable the Red Army to conduct multi-echeloned attacks on a vast scale, using the newly created tank armies to rip open the increasingly flimsy German frontlines time and again. As for individual tank engagements, Soviet commanders realized in 1943 that the new German tanks would inflict heavy losses on a local, tactical level, and they accepted these losses as the price of victory until better Soviet tanks could arrive in 1944.

Much of the historical writing about the role of the Panther and T-34 tanks has been dominated by simplistic generalizations rather than sober analysis of their actual combat performance. For decades, the Panther has often been praised as "the best tank of World War II," while the T-34, by 1943, has been criticized as inferior and capable of winning only through vast numbers. In particular, some German sources have depicted German weapons technology as superior, overcome solely by the avalanche of inferior Soviet weapons. However, the quality versus quantity argument tends to overlook the fact that any technical edge in warfare tends to be short lived and that the cost, in terms of pursuing a potential combat advantage, often means surrendering the production front to the enemy. In 1943, the Third Reich bet its future on the Panther while the Red Army played it safe and single-mindedly focused on fielding as many T-34s as possible. As always, the validation was on the battlefield, when the Panther would meet the T-34 in a duel for supremacy.

CHRONOLOGY

1933

Kharkov Locomotive Factory in USSR mounts an experimental diesel engine in a BT-5 light tank.

1937

November   KhPZ begins design work on A-20.

1938

May   KhPZ begins developing A-30 and A-32 variants.

1939

July   A-20 and A-32 prototypes begin testing.

Dec 19   T-32 is approved for production.

1940

March 17   Koshkin's demonstration of T-34 to Stalin.

March 31   Soviet Defense Ministry orders full-scale production of T-34.

Sept 15   First production T-34/76 Model 1940 built.

1941

February   First T-34/76 Model 1941 with F-34 gun built.

June 22   German invasion of USSR.

July   Rheinmetall in Germany begins developing a new, long 75mm gun and turret for next medium tank.

Oct 6   4th Panzer Division is defeated by Katukov's T-34s near Mtensk.

Nov 25   The German Army Ordnance Office sets a requirement for a new tank to defeat the Soviet T-34.

December   MAN and Daimler-Benz begin work on VK30.02 design.

A burning T-34/76 Model 1940 in testing at Kubinka. Soviet testing was realistic and included subjecting prototypes to antitank fire and Molotov cocktails. This testing ensured that the Red Army received a very durable weapon. (Kharkov Machine Building Design Bureau KMDB)

If ever there was an example that "haste makes waste" in warfare, it lies in the Panther development program. Instead of taking the time to ensure that a truly superior tank was fielded, bureaucrats at the Wa Pruef 6 and the Reich's Armaments Ministry succumbed to the temptation to rush a weapon into production without proper testing. Unlike the T-34, the Panther Ausf. D never underwent serious mobility or field trials, probably because it would have failed and embarrassed the Armaments Ministry. Guderian knew that the Panther was a loser, but he was silenced by Saur. Furthermore, the decision to add the Panther program on top of the existing tank and assault gun programs led to a harmful competition for resources that undermined the Third Reich's war effort. The Panther design did have several innovative features as well as the superb KwK 42 L/70 75mm gun and thick, sloped armor, but the vehicle as a whole fell short of Guderian's initial requirements. Given the Reich's increasing shortfalls in fuel production, the abandonment of a fuel-efficient diesel tank engine made no sense for the long-term war effort. The need for the Panther tank developed because of battlefield realities discovered in 1941, but German developers erred grievously by building a tank that essentially ignored these realities.

THE T-34/76

We will pay a big price if our vehicles are not battle worthy enough.
General Dmitri G. Pavlov speaking to Josef Stalin, March 18, 1940

In 1936, the Red Army (RKKA) had the largest fleet of tanks in the world, but its armor leaders had limited experience with using them in actual combat. Soviet tank designers had borrowed liberally from British and American tank designs of the early 1930s in order to produce the first generation of Soviet tanks. The bulk of Soviet tanks in 1936 were light T-26 and BT-5/7 series, weighing 10–13 tons, armed with a 45mm

Soviet T-34/76 Model 1941 medium tank with welded turret and rubber-ribbed road wheels. This tank was a great shock to the Germans in 1941 and prompted the development of the Panther. (Author's collection)

Mikhail I. Koshkin, Chief Designer at KhPZ during 1936–40. Koshkin was an aggressive, talented engineer whose vision of a well-rounded medium tank was invested in the T-34/76. Koshkin had to fight tooth and nail to get the T-34 built against the opposition of Marshal Voroshilov, who favored his son-in-law's KV-1 tank. (Kharkov Museum Machine Building Design Bureau KMDB)

gun, and having no more than 22mm of armor protection. The Soviets also had about 270 T-28 medium tanks and 60 T-35 heavy tanks. All Soviet tanks at this time employed petrol engines and were designed primarily as infantry support weapons.

The first major combat experience for Soviet armor occurred with the Russian intervention in the Spanish Civil War in October 1936. The Soviets sent 281 T-26B and 50 BT-5 light tanks to Spain to support the Republican forces. In general, the T-26B performed well in Spain, but the destruction of several tanks at the battle of Jarama in February 1937 by German 37mm AT guns caused the Soviet tankers to reconsider the thin armor on their tanks. General Dmitri G. Pavlov, the commander of the first Soviet armor sent to Spain and later head of the Soviet Armored Forces Directorate (GABTU), was particularly concerned about the flammability of the petrol-fueled T-26. Based upon early reports from Spain, the GABTU recommended developing a "shell-proof" tank that could withstand 37mm AT fire. In 1937, the Soviet Union had two main tank production centers: the Leningrad complex (Bolshevik, Kirov, and Voroshilov factories) and the Kharkov Locomotive Factory (KhPZ). GABTU initially recommended that the Leningrad factories design an improved variant of their T-26 light tank while KhPZ was ordered to design an improved BT-7. The result of this recommendation was the T-26S tank with a new conical turret and the BT-7M with an experimental V-2 diesel engine.

KhPZ had developed the BT-series "fast tanks" and the T-35 heavy tank. The chief engineer was Mikhail Koshkin, who took over in December 1936 after his predecessor had been arrested in the Stalinist purges. Koshkin had been a candy maker outside Moscow before the Russian Revolution, but he managed to get a technical education afterward and proved to be a brilliant engineer. Despite his technical prowess and vision, Koshkin was not above using his Communist Party connections to rise rapidly in the "Oboronka" (Russian slang for "military industrial complex"). Once at KhPZ, Koshkin was given the assignment of developing the improved BT-7M design as well as another variant known as the BT-SV that incorporated sloped armor. While Koshkin quickly completed these designs, he felt that such incremental improvements were too conservative to offer any real technological advantage. Instead, Koshkin saw the wheeled-tracked configuration utilized by the BT-series as a technical dead-end and preferred to develop a new tracked-only tank that would utilize the new diesel engine as well as sloped armor and a larger gun. KhPZ had been experimenting with diesel engines since 1933 and was on the verge of developing the first practical diesel engine for a tank. Koshkin's deputy, Alexsander Morozov, was responsible for developing the V-2 diesel engine from an earlier prototype. The V-2 was a huge breakthrough in tank engine development, allowing Koshkin to emphasize mobility and fire safety in the new design. In addition to using aluminum to reduce weight, the new V-2 offered better range, reliability, and 30 percent more power than any other contemporary tank engine.

Building a T-34/76 in the Urals. A T-34/76 in 1943 cost 135,000 rubles ($25,470) and required about 3,000 man-hours to complete. A Panther cost about 129,000 Reichsmarks ($51,600) and 55,000 man-hours to complete. (Tank Museum, Bovington)

By the fall of 1937, planners at GABTU began to realize that merely building improved variants of the T-26 and the BT-7 would not solve Soviet armor deficiencies. Even the improved versions were still thinly armored and undergunned vehicles that would soon be obsolete. GABTU recognized that Soviet armored forces needed completely new tank designs that would provide the firepower, protection, and mobility to triumph on a modern battlefield. Consequently, in November 1937 GABTU ordered KhPZ to begin design work on a new medium tank while the Voroshilov and Kirov factories in Leningrad were ordered to begin designing a new heavy tank. The new medium tank, designated the A-20, still reflected very conservative thinking, the requirement being for a 20-ton tank with a 45mm gun, 20mm of armor, and a wheel-track system – not really much of an improvement over the BT-7.

Six months later, the Soviet Defense Council of the Soviet People's Commissars (SNAKE) decided that the initial A-20 requirement was still vulnerable to the German 37mm Pak 36 and ordered KhPZ to develop a variant known as the A-30, which

MEDIUM TANK PROTOTYPES 1938				
BT-7M	A-20	A-32	T-34	Model 1940
Weight (metric tons)	14.6 (16.1 US tons)	18 (19.8 US tons)	19 (21 US tons)	26.3 (29 US tons)
Main Gun	45mm	45mm	76.2mm	76.2mm
Maximum Armor (mm)	22	25	30	45
Engine	V-2 diesel	V-2 diesel	V-2 diesel	V-2 diesel
Drive Configuration	Wheel-track	Wheel-track	Tracked	Tracked

The evolution of the Soviet medium tank: from left-to-right the A-8, the A-20, the T-34 Model 1940, and the T-34 M1941. Between 1938 and 1940, Koshkin doubled the weight of his tank design, increased the gun from 45mm to 76mm and increased armored protection from 22mm to 52mm. (Kharkov Morozov Machine Building Design Bureau KMDB)

increased armor to 30mm and increased the gun to 76.2mm. However, Koshkin and Morozov disliked the wheeled-tracked system used on the A-20, and on their own initiative they designed a further tracked-only variant known as the A-32 or T-32. General Pavlov, now head of GABTU, favored maintaining a capability to remove the tank's tracks and running it on its road wheels because this method offered superior operational mobility – a not insignificant factor in a large country with a poor internal transportation system. Thus, by the summer of 1938, KhPZ had three new medium tank prototypes in various stages of development: the A-20, A-30, and A-32.

At a conference on new tank designs in Moscow in August 1938, Josef Stalin took a personal interest in the medium tank prototypes. Like Hitler, Stalin got directly involved in major weapons projects. Although SNAKE favored the wheeled version of the A-30, Koshkin convinced Stalin that the tracked A-32 would have superior armored protection and that wheeled tanks had poor off-road mobility. Furthermore, when Koshkin pointed out to Stalin that the L-11 76.2mm gun would not fit in the A-30's small turret, Stalin ordered that project halted. However, the A-32 was opposed by Defense Commissar Marshal Klimenti Voroshilov, whose son in-law, Zhosif Kotin, was developing the KV-series heavy tank in Leningrad. Voroshilov and Kotin did not want KhPZ to develop a tank that was a direct competitor to the KV-series. By late 1938, KhPZ was pressing ahead with developing a wheeled-tracked A-20 to satisfy GABTU's initial requirement, but Koshkin was still developing the tracked-only A-32.

In July 1939, both prototypes of the A-20 and A-32 were completed by KhPZ and sent to Kubinka for evaluation. General Pavlov still preferred the A-20 because the smaller, less-complicated tank would be inexpensive to mass produce. However, there was no hiding from Stalin the fact that the A-20 performed poorly in its off-road mobility tests when used in its wheeled mode and that the A-32 clearly had superior firepower and armored protection. Stalin was unconcerned about cost issues, but he wanted a medium tank that could be built in large numbers. When Pavlov and Voroshilov suggested that the A-32 was too complex for KhPZ to manufacture in quantity, Stalin agreed to defer on an immediate decision. Stalin did not want another T-28 or T-35 that could only be built in token numbers. For the next several months, the final decision was left floating in bureaucratic limbo, pending more testing with the prototypes. At the same time, the Kirovsky heavy tank project was finally making progress, and the KV-1 design was approved for production in August 1939. GABTU agreed that both the new medium tank and the KV-1 would utilize the new V-2 engine, sloped armor, and either the L-11 or F-34 76mm tank gun.

The realities of actual warfare also had a profound influence upon the development of the T-34 tank. On November 30, 1939, the Soviet Union attacked Finland, but in the first week the Soviets lost 80 tanks to a handful of Finnish AT guns. Furthermore, the Soviet 45mm tank gun proved completely ineffective at neutralizing Finnish bunkers. As Soviet tank losses mounted in Finland, it became apparent to GABTU that the new medium tank needed better protection and firepower. On December 9, SNAKE selected the A-32 as the new medium tank and cancelled the A-20. The Defense Council ordered KhPZ to immediately build 220 A-32 tanks. Although this seemed like a victory for Koshkin, Voroshilov had not agreed to authorize production of Koshkin's latest version of the new tank, known as the T-34. This variant was 38 percent heavier than the A-32 and had a maximum of 45mm of sloped armor, which Koshkin felt would ensure the tank's invulnerability to 37mm fire. Instead, Voroshilov demanded that the T-34 should undergo further "testing" before he would authorize production. Apparently, Voroshilov hindered the T-34's development in order to boost the prestige that he would gain when his son-in-law's KV-1 tank entered service in spring 1940.

Koshkin was undaunted by Voroshilov's meddling and was unwilling to see his revolutionary design pushed aside. Instead of simply sulking in Kharkov, Koshkin ventured upon a dramatic demonstration by driving the first two unarmed T-34 prototypes to Moscow. Between March 5 and 17, Koshkin and two crews drove the T-34s roughly 700km from Kharkov to Moscow, where the tanks were presented to Stalin. On this grueling road test, Koshkin contracted the pneumonia that would kill him six months later. Voroshilov, who was present at the demonstration, was visibly upset by this stunt, but he could not deny the T-34's qualities. After showing the T-34 to Stalin, both prototypes were driven to the Kubinka test area where the tanks' sloped armor successfully withstood fire from 45mm AT guns. The T-34s also conducted mobility trials at Kubinka with a Pz III purchased from Germany.

A prototype T-32 medium tank, armed with the L-11 76.2mm gun. Koshkin built this prototype in 1939 on his own initiative and it led to the improved T-34 design. (Kharkov Morozov Machine Building Design Bureau KMDB)

In order to further demonstrate the new tank's mechanical reliability, both prototypes were then driven back to KhPZ via Smolensk and Kiev, completing a 2,900km (1,802-mile) road test. In late March, one prototype was sent by rail to the Finnish front, where it demonstrated that its L-11 76.2mm gun could demolish captured Finnish bunkers. On March 31, 1940, the Defense Ministry approved full-scale production of the T-34 at KhPZ and the Stalingrad Tractor Works (STZ).

This type of road test was far beyond the abilities of any other contemporary tank and proved the inherent robustness of the T-34's diesel engine. However, the road test revealed a tendency for the engine to overheat and it also showed that the steering controls were rather primitive. The transmission designed by Morozov – similar to the one used on the BT-series light tanks – proved problematic for much of the T-34's early career. GABTU was also concerned that the two-man turret on the T-34 was too small and cramped compared to the three-man turret on the Pz III. Thus, General Pavlov ordered the KhPZ to address these improvements to the basic T-34 design before proceeding with mass production. KhPZ recommended two potential variants: the A-41 with a three-man turret and the A-43, also known as the T-34M.

As KhPZ began to prepare for series production of the T-34/76 in late 1940, it had to integrate key components such as the L-11 76.2mm gun from the Kirovski Works and V-2 diesel engines from Factory #75 in Kharkov. Although SNAKE increased the order for T-34s to 600 after the fall of France, KhPZ's pace of development slowed during the summer of 1940 because it had to work on improving the basic design as well as planning for short-term improvements.

By September 15, seven months after the first prototypes appeared, three production Model 1940 T-34/76 tanks were completed. However, the T-34/76's development was plagued during the winter of 1940–41 by bureaucratic interference and material shortages. Therefore, KhPZ was only able to complete 115 of the planned 600 tanks

A Soviet T-34/76 Model 1943 from the summer of that year. Most T-34s arrived from the factory without any exterior markings and turret numbers were rarely used in typical units at this phase of the war. However, Guards Tanks units were often encouraged to display numbers, slogans and Soviet symbology on their turrets for propaganda purposes.

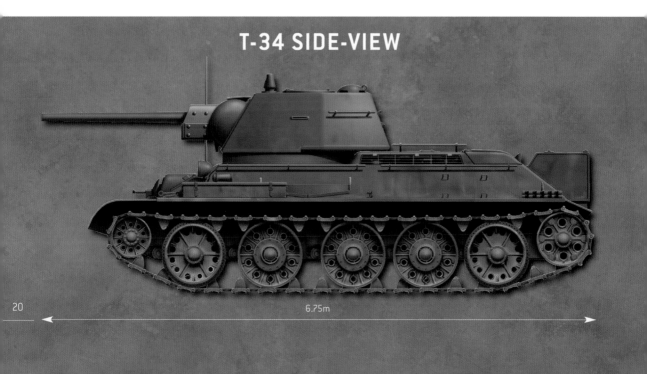

T-34 SIDE-VIEW

6.75m

for 1940. Marshal Grigory Kulik, Commander of the Artillery Directorate, curtailed deliveries of the L-11 gun while Vorishilov and Pavlov argued that T-34 production should be suspended until the T-34M variant was ready. With plans for a new turret, torsion bar suspension, and a new V-5 diesel engine, the T-34M was indeed superior to the basic T-34. Several prototypes of the T-34M were nearing completion in June 1941, but this advanced design would not be ready for full-scale production until 1942. In warfare, the "best" is often the enemy of the "good," and the T-34M wasted a great deal of design and production energy on a tank that would not be ready for some time. Given the tendency for Soviet committees to suggest new variants and to push "pet theories," it is almost a miracle that any T-34 tanks were available in 1941.

The initial T-34/76 Model 1940 weighed in at 26.3 tons and was armed with the L-11 76.2mm gun. Koshkin viewed the L-11 as an interim weapon until the new F-34 76.2mm gun became available, and this gun, as well as a cast turret with thicker armor, was earmarked for the Model 1941 version of the T-34/76. However, Koshkin died in September 1940, leaving the Model 1941 without a firm advocate. (Morozov succeeded him at KhPZ.) When the improved T-34/76 Model 1941 with the F-34 gun and turret began production in February 1941, GABTU and SNAKE allowed the outmoded Model 1940 to remain in production as well. On May 5, SNAKE increased the order for T-34 tanks to 2,800 and authorized production of the upgraded T-34M.

By the time of the German invasion of the Soviet Union on June 22, the KhPZ and the Stalingrad Tank Factory had built about 1,226 T-34/76 tanks for the Red Army, which was roughly an equal mix of Model 1940 and Model 1941. However, at the start of Operation *Barbarossa*, only 5 percent of the Red Army's tanks were T-34s and 2 percent were KV heavy tanks, meaning that the bulk of Soviet armored forces were still composed of obsolescent light tanks. Approximately 982 T-34/76 and 466 KV-1 tanks were deployed in the Western military districts at the start of the

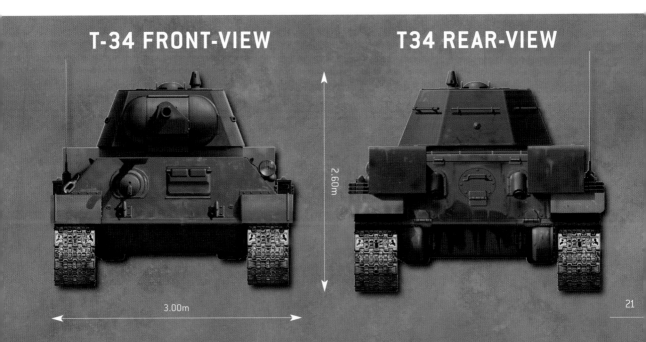

T-34 FRONT-VIEW   **T34 REAR-VIEW**

2.60m

3.00m

invasion. Yet despite all its technical promise, the initial combat debut of the T-34/76 in 1941 was a disaster due to inadequate training and skimpy logistics. The T-34's baptism of fire occurred in Lithuania near Rassinye, when about 50 T-34s from the 3rd Tank Regiment/2nd Tank Division mounted a clumsy counterattack against the spearheads of the 1st and 6th Panzer Divisions between June 24 and 25. Although the T-34s caused a brief panic when 37mm AT guns failed to penetrate their armor, the Soviet attack was stopped by a few 88mm flak guns.

General Pavlov had left GABTU to command the Western Front just before the start of the war. Pavlov's command included the 6th Mechanized Corps, one of the Red Army's strongest armored formations with 238 T-34 tanks. Unfortunately for Pavlov, the 6th Mechanized Corps had no armor-piercing (AP) rounds for the T-34s and only one load of fuel per tank. Due to security concerns, few T-34 crewmen had actually been trained. The best-designed tank in the world is merely scrap iron if it does not have ammunition, fuel, or a trained crew, and that was the condition of virtually all the T-34 units in the summer of 1941. The 6th Mechanized Corps and all its vital T-34s were annihilated in the first two weeks of the war without accomplishing anything of consequence. By early July, about half the available T-34 and KV-1 tanks had been lost as the Soviet border armies were destroyed, and most of the remaining pre-war T-34s were lost in the Kiev Pocket. When Pavlov's command was wiped out in the Minsk Pocket, he was recalled to Moscow and executed.

Once the extent of Soviet armor losses in the opening battles became apparent, the Soviet National Defense Committee (GKO) decided that quantity, not quality, was the key to victory. Production of the T-34M was cancelled. The Model 1941 T-34/76 became the standard model, and another 1,886 were built in the last half of 1941. However, a total of 2,300 were lost. Once the KhPZ was relocated at Nizhni Tagil in the Urals, Morozov began work on designing the T-34 Model 1942. The main emphasis on the Model 1942 was to simplify the design in order to increase production. This result was admirably achieved, although some of the T-34s were built with inferior or incomplete components. The only significant change in the Model 1942 was an increase in the maximum frontal armor to 65mm, thereby adding two tons to the vehicle's weight. Problems with the KV-1 heavy tank also forced the Red Army to place greater reliance on the T-34 because it was essentially the only effective Soviet design in production. A total of 12,553 T-34s were built in 1942 but 6,500 were lost – a disappointing 51 percent loss rate.

In mid-1942, Morozov began designing the T-34 Model 1943, which would use the newly developed hexagonal turret with two hatches instead of the one large hatch on earlier models. The new turret also had slightly thicker armor of 70mm, but the poor visibility problem was not corrected until mid-1943 when a cupola was introduced. The T-34 Model 1943 would comprise the bulk of T-34s available for the campaigns in the Ukraine in 1943. The Model 1943 was a good tank, but it indicated that Soviet tank design had stagnated in the 18 months since the war began: the T-34 was still armed with a 76.2mm gun and armor that was no longer immune to the improved German AT guns. The Red Army would have to fight for the remainder of 1943 with the T-34/76, no longer enjoying a major technical advantage over German tanks. However, the model was at least finally available in quantity.

THE STRATEGIC SITUATION

After the surrender of the German 6th Army at Stalingrad on February 2, 1943, it became obvious to the OKH, if not Hitler, that the war in the East was turning against Germany. Yet despite the catastrophic situation facing the Ostheer (German Army in the East) in southern Russia in early 1943, the Germans still had some hope of regaining the initiative. A bold counterattack by German commander Erich von Manstein from February 18 to March 20 virtually destroyed the overextended Soviet 3rd Tank Army, retaking Kharkov and pushing back the Red Army from the approaches to the Dnepr River. With the spring thaw in late March 1943, an operational pause ensued for several months, giving both sides time to rebuild their depleted armor units and to make plans for future offensives.

OPERATION *ZITADELLE*

Hitler realized that with his limited resources, a major summer offensive was no longer possible. He did hope, however, that bold, local offensives could inflict punishing losses and prevent the Red Army from seizing the initiative. Generaloberst Kurt Zeitzler, OKH chief of staff, issued a plan named *Zitadelle* on April 15, that envisioned encircling and destroying Soviet forces in the Kursk salient. Zeitzler hoped to repeat Von Manstein's successful March 1943 counterattack but with better equipment and on a bigger scale. Realizing that the Soviets now held a significant numerical advantage,

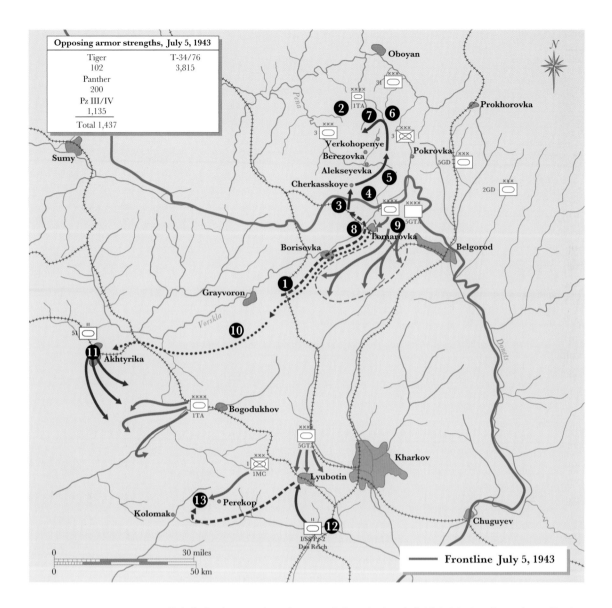

Frontline July 5, 1943

Zeitzler's plan was based on regaining the battlefield initiative through qualitative superiority provided by the new Panthers, Tigers, and Ferdinands heavy tanks. The attack was originally planned to begin on May 3, but Karl-Otto Saur, Speer's deputy, succeeded in convincing Zeitzler and Hitler that the offensive should wait until June when significant numbers of Panthers and Tigers would arrive at the front. Serious technical problems with the Panther resulted in the postponement of the operation several times. Finally, realizing that either Soviet or Allied offensives were imminent, Hitler set July 5 as the start date for *Zitadelle*.

Operationally, Zeitzler opted for the proven method of a pincer attack by Army Group Center's 9th Army and Army Group South's 4th Panzer Army to cut off the six Soviet armies within the Kursk salient. *Zitadelle* was unusual in that it committed the bulk of Germany's armor to several narrow attack sectors, leaving few tanks on

MAP KEY: JULY–SEPTEMBER 1943

1. July 1–3 : 51st and 52nd Panzer Battalions arrive by rail near Borisovka. Around 20 Panthers break down during a 35km road march to assembly area northwest of Tomarovka.

2. Soviet 1st TA has 3rd MC, 6th TC, and 31st TC with 500 T-34 tanks in first echelon of Soviet defense. 230 T-34 tanks are in reserve.

3. 0815 July 5: 39th Panzer begins attack north toward Cherkasskoye with about 166 Panthers. Soviet counterattack is repulsed but the Panthers are stalled crossing a ravine.

4. 1040 July 6: 39th Panzer reassembles around Cherkasskoye and continues attacking. Only about 50 Panthers are still operational. The attack is slowed by an antitank ditch.

5. 0840 July 7: 39th Panzer continues attack runs into prepared defenses of 3rd Mechanized Corps on Pena River. The Panthers are stopped by a mine and wire obstacles at a ravine and come under deadly crossfire from about 60 dug-in T-34s from the 1st and 3rd Mechanized Bdes. The Panthers "freeze" in the Soviet kill sack and 27 are knocked out, including some by flank shots from T-34s. However, the Panthers' superior gunnery is able to take a toll of the T-34s as well, and the Soviets pull back around 1500 hours. The Panthers continue the attack against the 112th Tank Bde. During the day, the Panthers destroyed about 30 T-34s. This is the first major Panther vs. T-34 engagement of the war.

6. July 12: 39th Panzer continues attacking toward Verkhopen'ye with only 10–15 Panthers operational. Panthers engage counterattacking T-34s from 1st Guard Tank Bde and 200th Tank Bde with some success.

7. 0500 July 14: 39th Panzer launches one last attack to contain Soviet 10th TC counteroffensive west of Verkhopen'ye, but six Panthers are destroyed and ten more breakdown. A total of 56 Panthers have been lost since the start of *Zitadelle*, but the Germans claim that the Panthers destroyed over 200 Soviet T-34s.

8. July 17–19: 39th Panzer is disbanded at Tomarovka. 51st Panzer hands over all its remaining Panthers to 52nd Battalion. 51st receives 96 new Panthers while in the rear. 52nd Panzer is attached to 19th Panzer Div. On August 6 51st Panzer Battalion returns to 4th Panzer Army.

9. 0500 August 3: Soviets launch Operation *Rumantsyev* counteroffensive; 1st TA and 5th Guards TA attack with about 800 T-34s on a narrow 12km front between Tomarovka and Belgorod. Within two days, the Soviet armor has ripped a huge hole in the German defenses. The 52nd Panzer defends Tomarovka with 27 Panthers and destroys 7 T-34s from 6th TC.

10. August 6–8 : 52nd Panzer retreats down Vorskla River valley, fighting running battles with 1st TA, destroying about 40 T-34s but is reduced to 11 Panthers.

11. August 9–26 : 51st Panzer fights a series of battles around Achtyrka against the Soviet 1st TA and helps in isolating the 4th Guards TC. In two weeks of heavy fighting, the battalion loses 36 Panthers and 24 KIA, but the 1st TA is severely damaged.

12. August 22 : SS Das Reich's Panther battalion arrives as Kharkov is falling and counterattacks 5th Guards TA at Lyubotin, destroying 53 tanks. The next day, seven more T-34s from 29th TC are destroyed by Panthers near Lyubotin.

13. September 12–13 : SS Das Reich Panthers destroy 35 T-34s from 219th Tank Brigade (1 MC) in Kolomak area with no losses.

---

the rest of the Eastern Front. On July 1, Army Group South had a total of 23 panzer battalions and nine assault gun or panzerjaeger battalions with a total of about 1,850 tanks and assault guns, or about 60 percent of all German armor on the Eastern Front.

Operation *Zitadelle* was a seriously flawed plan that ignored Soviet improvements in defensive capabilities and simply assumed that the reinforced panzer divisions could defeat anything in their path. Zeitzler and Hitler allowed their optimism about the Panther and Tiger tanks to shape their belief that Soviet quantitative superiority was irrelevant and a decisive victory could be achieved.

Despite Saur's promises to Hitler, the Panthers of the 39th Panzer Regiment barely arrived in time for the Kursk offensive. The battalions arrived by rail between July 1 and 4, and the trail elements did not reach their assembly areas until the day before the attack began. There was little or no time to brief the battalion commanders, and the junior leaders were virtually in the dark about the mission or objectives. The battle plan was amazingly simplistic and virtually ignored the terrain and the enemy defenses. As part of the 48th Panzer Corps' attack toward Oboyan, the 39th Panzer Regiment would attack with Panzer Regiment Grossdeutschland and smash through the Soviet lines in a great armored fist with over 300 tanks deployed on a very narrow attack sector.

OPERATION *RUMANTSYEV*

Soviet intelligence had provided warnings of the impending German offensive against the Kursk salient and for once, the Stavka (the General Headquarters of the Soviet Union) was able to convince Stalin that it was better to defeat the German attack and then switch to the counteroffensive. The three months of relative quiet from April to June 1943 allowed the Red Army to replenish and rebuild its depleted tank units and create significant reserve forces. The Voronezh front, under General Nikolai Vatutin, was tasked with stopping the 4th Panzer Army's offensive and depleting its armored spearheads in a series of grinding battles. Vatutin's main armored force was Lieutenant General Katukov's 1st Tank Army, which had about 500 T-34s. Katukov intended to use many of his T-34s and AT guns from dug-in, mutually supporting positions to fix and wear down the German panzer wedges while keeping some T-34 battalions to conduct flanking attacks as the Germans advanced into the Soviet defensive belts. Once the German offensive was halted, the Soviets would commit their reserves from Colonel-General Ivan Konev's Steppe Front, which included the 5th Guards Tank Army under Lieutenant-General Pavel Rotmistrov. Together, the Soviet Voronezh and steppe fronts that opposed the 4th Panzer Army and Army Detachment Kempf, a panzer unit, possessed a total of 123 tank battalions with about 3,350 tanks, including about 2,300 T-34s. For the first time in the war, the Soviets would be able to mass a large force of their best armor and about 50 percent of their available tanks.

Before the battle of Kursk began, Marshal Georgi Zhukov envisioned that the Voronezh front would launch the main counteroffensive toward Kharkov as soon as the German offensive had culminated, but Soviet tank losses were more serious than expected during the defensive phase and it required two weeks to repair battle-damaged vehicles. On July 24, the Stavka ordered Vatutin and Konev to begin detailed planning for Operation *Rumantsyev*, which was to begin in ten days. Vatutin's Voronezh front would attack with the 1st Tank Army and 5th Guards Tank Army to envelop Kharkov from the west while other armies assaulted from north and east. The operation's intent was to seize Kharkov and breach the 4th Panzer Army lines in about two weeks. Once Kharkov was recovered, Zhukov and Stalin anticipated offensives by the southern and southwest fronts to clear the Donbas in late August and reaching the Dnepr River at Zaporozh'ye in September. Meanwhile, the Voronezh and steppe fronts would drive west toward the Dnepr River at Kremenchug. The chances of Operation *Rumantsyev* succeeding were enhanced by the Soviet ability to maintain large armored forces on other fronts and to mount successful diversionary attacks. While the Germans had to strip virtually the entire Eastern Front of armor in order to mount *Zitadelle*, the Soviet southwest and southern fronts still had over 1,600 tanks available.

TECHNICAL SPECIFICATIONS

The engine of the panzer is its weapon just as much as the cannon.
Generaloberst Heinz Guderian

ARMOR PROTECTION

Both the Soviets and the Germans sought to develop a medium tank that could withstand a hit from contemporary AT guns. However, it was easier to increase the size of AT weapons than it was to increase armor on tanks, which meant that by 1943 it was accepted that only heavy tanks could carry enough armor to defeat weapons in the 75–85mm range. The introduction of sloped armor on the T-34/76 succeeded in increasing armored protection while keeping the vehicle's gross weight within reason. Wa Pruf 6 was quick to realize that all new German tank designs should incorporate at least some sloped armor.

The armor on the T-34/76 was initially designed to withstand hits from AT guns in the 37–50mm range, but when the Germans introduced the long 75mm KwK 40 L43 gun on their Pz IV Ausf. F2 in May 1942, the comfortable margin of safety on the Soviet tank disappeared. Suddenly, German tanks armed with the new long-barreled guns could destroy T-34s at 1,000m instead of being limited to only point-blank attacks. Furthermore, from 1940 to 1943 the T-34's armor was only increased from a maximum of 45mm to 70mm, but at least 90mm of frontal armor was needed to provide some degree of protection against the KwK 40. Additionally, the quality of Soviet armor plate was often poor, and the nickel content used to harden steel plate – typically 1 to 1.5 percent – was less than on German tanks. The weaker Soviet armor plate tended to spall, or break off in chips, more easily when hit, and metal splinters caused the majority of Soviet tanker casualties. By the time of *Zitadelle*, the T-34/76 had lost its edge in armored protection and was now vulnerable to destruction at long range from a wide variety of German weapons, including the new Panthers and Tigers.

Although the Panther's sloped armor is often described as revolutionary for German tank design, this characterization is misleading. The frontal armor protection on the Panther Ausf. D was thicker than the Pz IV Ausf. H, having 100mm at 12° on the turret front (instead of 50mm) and a sloped glacis plate that was 80mm thick at 55° (versus 80mm at 78°). While the 100mm-thick gun mantlet was generally impervious to most AP rounds in 1943, Soviet AP rounds fired from close range during *Zitadelle* cracked the mantlet on at least three Panthers from the 52nd Panzer Battalion. Moreover, the side and rear armor on the Panther was only marginally thicker than the Pz IV Ausf. H. The Panther had 40mm of hull side armor (versus 30mm), the Panther's turret side armor was 45mm at 25° (instead of 50mm at 79°), and rear armor was 40–45mm (instead of 20–30mm). In fact, the Panther was quite vulnerable to flanking fire, which often ignited the fuel tanks.

Ostensibly, the Panther's armor was designed to meet Guderian's specification for a tank that could withstand the T-34's 76.2mm gun. Based upon examination of captured T-34s, the Germans were aware that the F-34 gun was capable of penetrating up to 63mm of sloped armor at 1,000m. Thus, Wa Pruf 6 should have realized that the Panther's 40–45mm of side armor was insufficient to withstand

PANTHER GUN

1. Muzzle brake
2. 75mm Kw.K 42 L/70 gun
3. Mantlet
4. MG 34 machine-gun
5. Turret lifting ring
6. Extractor fan
7. Vane sight
8. Cupola
9. Cupola vision block
10. Recoil guard
11. Breech ring
12. 75mm ammunition stowage
13. Empty shell case bin
14. Gunner's seat
15. Rotary base junction
16. Turret floor
17. Elevating handwheel
18. Counterbalance
19. Hydraulic traverse motor
20. Binocular sighting telescope

flanking shots from T-34s at normal combat ranges. While the Panther's frontal armor was as good as the Tiger's, its side armor offered only a modest improvement over the Pz IV. Hitler realized that the Panther wasn't well armored enough, and he kept demanding that Wa Pruf 6 increase the level of armored protection. In response, Wa Pruf 6 developed the *Schuerzen* armored side skirts for the Panther and began work on a more heavily armored variant, the Panther II. While the Panther II offered 60mm of side armor, the increased armor raised the Panther's weight to over 50 tons. After several months of technical discussion between Wa Pruf 6 and MAN, the Panther II design was shelved in May 1943, and the decision was made to incorporate some of its features into future versions of the Panther. As for the side skirt armor, this *ad hoc* measure proved to be of limited value since most of these broke off under

SPECIFICATIONS: PANTHER AUSF. A

General
Production run: Ausf. D: January–September 1943
Ausf. A: August 1943–July 1944
Vehicles produced: Ausf. D: 842
Ausf. A: 2,200
Combat weight: 44.8 tons (metric)
Crew: Five (tank commander, gunner, loader, driver, radio operator)

Dimensions
Overall length: 8.86mm
Hull length: 7.10m
Width: 3.42m (with side skirts)
Height: 2.95m

Armour
Hull front: 80mm (at 55 degrees)
Hull sides: 40mm (at 50 degrees)
Hull rear: 40mm (at 30 degrees)
Hull roof: 16mm (at 90 degrees)
Turret front: 100mm (at 12 degrees)
Turret sides: 45mm (at 25 degrees)
Turret rear: 45mm (at 25 degrees)
Turret roof: 16mm (at 90 degrees)

Armament
Main gun: 1 x 75mm KwK 42/L70
Secondary: 2 x 7.92mm MG 34
Main gun rate of fire: 3–5rpm

Ammunition stowage
Main: 79 rounds (typically 40 rounds PzGr. 39/42 APC and 39 rounds SpGr. 42 HE)
Secondary: 4,200 rounds

Communications
Fu-5 transmitter/receiver; intercom

Motive power
Engine: Maybach HL 230 P 30 12-cylinder petrol engine
Power: 600hp at 2,500rpm
Fuel capacity: 720 liters
Power-to-weight ratio: 15.5hp/ton

Performance
Ground pressure: 0.73kg/cm²
Maximum road speed: 55kph
Maximum cross-country speed: 30kph
Operational range (road): 250km
Operational range (cross-country): 100km
Fuel consumption (road): 2.8 liters/km
Fuel consumption (cross-country): 7.3 liters/km
Cost: RM 129,000 ($51, 600)

1. Panzergranate 39/42 (AP)
2. Sprenggranaten 42 (HE)

combat conditions. Thus, the Panther Ausf. D and Ausf. A models that fought in the Ukraine in 1943 were too lightly armored and did not meet Guderian's 1941 specifications. Overall, the Panther Ausf. D clearly had better frontal armored protection than the T-34/76 Model 1943, but the level of protection still fell far short of what was needed.

FIREPOWER

An AP round can achieve various levels of penetration on the battlefield, depending upon the range and the striking angle. A round can achieve target destruction by physically penetrating the armor, but it may also inflict serious damage by causing the armor to spall inside. In general, fewer than 50 percent of actual hits in 1943 either knocked out or destroyed a tank, and only about 25 percent of tanks that were immobilized were permanently lost.

The T-34/76 Model 1943 typically carried 75 OF-350 HE-Frag and 25 BR-350A APHE rounds (including four tungsten-cored BR-350P rounds after October 1943). The Panther usually carried 40 rounds of Pzgr. 39/42 APC and 39 rounds of Sprgr. 42 HE ammunition. Soviet gunners tended to fire a lot of ammunition – often half their basic load in a single engagement – while German gunners had to be more conservative because their ammunition resupply was not always reliable.

Like its sloped armor, the T-34/76's F-34 gun was designed for the battlefield of 1941, not 1943. The standard BR-350A 76.2mm AP round used on the T-34 fired a steel projectile with a muzzle velocity of 662m/s (1,480mph). This round could

A Soviet propaganda photo of a T-34 unit liberating a Ukrainian village. The reality of liberation was that advance guard Soviet tank units were often forced to beg or steal food from the locals – "known as grandmother's rations" – since their own supply lines were far in the rear. (Courtesy of the Central Museum of the Armed Forces Moscow)

penetrate the Panther's side armor out to about 1,000m, but it could only penetrate the glacis armor at about 300m and could not penetrate the turret frontal armor. The BR-350P APDS round introduced in October 1943 could damage the Panther's frontal armor at ranges under 100m but could not achieve reliable target destruction. The T-34/76's firepower was also handicapped by the lack of a dedicated gunner, forcing the tank commander to first acquire the target with the PTK periscope and then switch to the TMFD gunner's sight. The TMFD was inferior to the Panther's TFZ12 sight, having a narrower field of view and less magnification. However, the T-34/76 did have one advantage over the Panther in terms of firepower, and that was its turret traverse speed. The T-34/76 had a turret traverse speed of 30° per second, or 12 seconds for a full rotation, which was five times faster than the Panther Ausf. D and 50 percent faster than the Panther Ausf. A. Faster turret rotation allowed T-34 gunners to redirect fire more quickly, particularly at close range.

The 75mm KwK 40 L43 gun on the Pz IV F2 fired an AP round with a muzzle velocity of 740m/s (1,655mph) that could

A Panther Ausf. D crew replacing two damaged track blocks on Panther "134" in the fall of 1943. This tank has been towed back to a railhead, apparently after receiving mine damage. Note opened access panels on hull rear for adjusting track tension. (Nik Cornish WH839)

penetrate up to 87mm of armor at 1,000m, easily guaranteeing destruction of the T-34. The 75mm KwK 42 L70 developed for the Panther was an even more powerful gun that fired a standard AP round that could penetrate 111mm of armor at 1,000m, far more armor than carried on any existing Soviet tank. Furthermore, the tungsten-cored Panzergranate 40/42 round had an even better performance, with an 1,120m/s muzzle velocity and the ability to penetrate 150mm of armor at 1,000m. With the excellent TFZ12 sight, Panther gunners could theoretically engage targets out to 3,000m, although commanders usually forbade firing at very long ranges in order not to waste rounds. Thus, the Panther's main gun was well designed for long-range killing, and it clearly was superior to the F-34 gun, but it offered few significant advantages over the KwK 40. In firepower, the Panther met Guderian's requirement, and it did outclass the T-34, but it should also be remembered that the trade-offs for gaining this superior gun were significant. The larger KwK 42 meant a bigger turret and, therefore, a wider hull, resulting in greater weight and less mobility.

MOBILITY

The T-34/76 was built around its V-2 diesel engine, and the automotive design was so sound that its successor, the T-34/85, was able to keep the same chassis. While the T-34's armor protection and firepower advantages had largely disappeared by 1943, its superior mobility was clearly demonstrated when 5th Guards Tank Army was able to move its T-34s 300km on their own tracks to the front between July 7–9 and still had about 90 percent of its tanks operational. No Panther unit could ever have moved this distance without losing most of its tanks to mechanical breakdowns.

Although Guderian asked for a tank with superior mobility, Wa Pruf 6 and MAN had different conceptions about what this meant. The design team's fixation on torsion bar suspension and quick dismissal of equipping the Panther with a diesel engine led to the development of a tank that essentially ignored the T-34's mobility advantages. While the T-34 was a 30-ton tank equipped with rear wheel drive and a diesel engine, the Panther was a 45-ton tank equipped with front wheel drive and a petrol engine. Amazingly, Wa Pruf 6 even overlooked the simple efficiency of the T-34's Christie suspension and instead opted for complex interleaved road wheel running gear, which proved to quickly clog up with mud in the soft fields of the Ukraine. Furthermore, replacing an inner road wheel on the Panther was more difficult because it required removing the adjacent road wheels as well. Obviously, the engineers who designed the Panther put little thought into how the vehicle would be operated or maintained under field conditions.

Some of the T-34's advantages in mobility declined as new models added weight but without increasing engine output. The introduction of the new hexagonal turret in 1942 added about two tons to the T-34's overall weight. In terms of statistical comparison, the Panther Ausf. D did appear to have equal or better mobility to the T-34, having lower ground pressure and better road speed. However, in reality, the

The agility of the T-34/76 constantly astonished the Germans. Soviet tankers often drove their vehicles at maximum speed to cross the German "kill zone" as rapidly as possible. (From the fonds of the RGAKFD in Krasnogorsk)

Panther could only move faster than the T-34 once it reached seventh gear, which was unlikely to occur under combat conditions. In tactical driving using third gear, the Panther was considerably slower than the T-34, being able to achieve only 13kph (8mph) versus 29kph (18mph). Certainly, one of the biggest problems with the Panther Ausf. D and A models was the fuel-guzzling character of its Maybach HL 230 engine, which required almost double the amount of fuel to go 1km as a Pz IV and nearly four times as much as a T-34. As the Wehrmacht began to run seriously short of fuel in late 1943, the Panther's poor fuel efficiency would further degrade its operational and tactical mobility.

The rugged and simplistic construction of the T-34 paid off with an operational reliability rate of around 70–90 percent in most Soviet armor units in 1943. In contrast, no German panzer unit equipped with Panther Ausf. D or A model tanks was able to sustain an operation readiness rate above 35 percent for any sustained period in 1943. Far more Panthers were lost to mechanical failure in 1943 than to enemy action, while the opposite was true for T-34s. Although the Panther's AK 7-200 transmission was nominally superior to the clumsy transmission on the T-34, about 5 percent broke down within 100km and over 90 percent within 1,500km in combat. The final drive on the Panther Ausf. D was so weak that the tank could not even turn while it was backing up, which occurred frequently in the retreat to the Dnepr River. Its two fuel pumps were probably the biggest mobility weakness in the Panther Ausf. D because they were prone to leaks and caused serious engine fires. At least three Panthers were destroyed by fuel pump-caused fires during *Zitadelle*, and a high proportion of mechanical breakdowns was caused by this troublesome component. Nor did this problem go away after Kursk: the initial batch of Panther Ausf. A tanks that were handed over to the SS-Leibstandarte in Italy in September 1943 were so problematic that every one was rejected for service.

The Panther's poor mobility forced the Wehrmacht to move units around by rail and get them as close to the front as possible before unloading. Throughout 1943, the Panther was essentially tied to conducting all major movements by rail, including the equally short-legged Tiger, and units could not even move 100km without significant losses. Thus, the Panther did not meet Guderian's requirement for a tank with superior mobility, and it was the T-34's continued advantage in mobility and reliability that contributed greatly to the Soviet victory in the Ukraine in 1943.

Panthers "415" and "732" from the 52nd Panzer Battalion abandoned at the Borisovka repair depot on August 6, 1943. Although the Germans attempted to destroy the vehicles, many Panthers were left virtually intact. (Courtesy of the Central Museum of the Armed Forces Moscow)

COMMUNICATIONS

The standard Panther Ausf. D was equipped with an intercom system that allowed all five crewmembers to communicate in combat. A Fu 5 transmitter and a UHF receiver were also standard equipment. Normally, a platoon leader would operate with his platoon frequency on the Fu 5 and monitor his company frequency on the UHF receiver. The command versions the Panther would typically carry were a long-range Fu 7 or Fu 8 transmitter to communicate with higher headquarters, a Fu 5 to talk with subordinate commanders, and an additional receiver to monitor other radio nets. Soviet tankers were quick to notice the extra antennas on command Panthers, and these were usually marked as high-priority targets. While about 80 percent of T-34s were equipped with the 9R AM radio by late 1943, the radio did not function well on the move, and company and battalion commanders were limited to the same short-range system. The T-34's intercom system was also limited to only the commander and the driver, leaving the other two crew members virtually isolated. The T-34's intercom was so unreliable that most tank commanders preferred to tap with their boots on their drivers' left or right shoulder to indicate direction. Simple sign language was used to communicate with the loader. Overall, the Panther enjoyed a communications advantage over the T-34 at both the crew and unit levels, which contributed to some German tactical successes. However, the hasty manner in which Panthers were often thrown into combat in the Ukraine in 1943 – often straight off the rail cars they arrived on – led to units getting no chance to establish functioning radio nets.

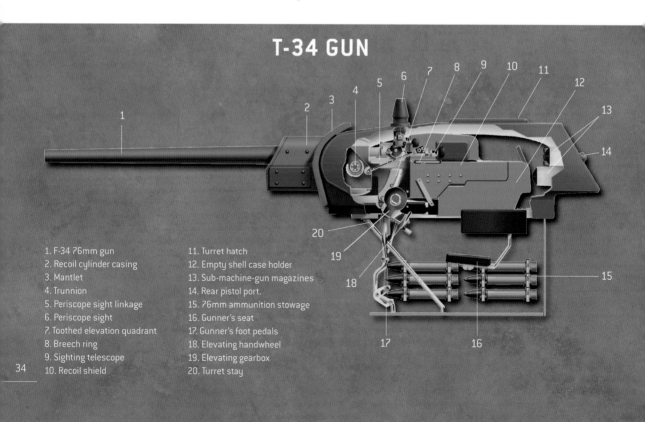

T-34 GUN

1. F-34 76mm gun
2. Recoil cylinder casing
3. Mantlet
4. Trunnion
5. Periscope sight linkage
6. Periscope sight
7. Toothed elevation quadrant
8. Breech ring
9. Sighting telescope
10. Recoil shield
11. Turret hatch
12. Empty shell case holder
13. Sub-machine-gun magazines
14. Rear pistol port.
15. 76mm ammunition stowage
16. Gunner's seat
17. Gunner's foot pedals
18. Elevating handwheel
19. Elevating gearbox
20. Turret stay

OVERALL TECHNICAL ASSESSMENT

Over the years, the PzKpfw V Panther has been commonly described as "the best tank of World War II" but such simplistic assessments have been made with little regard for the Panther's actual capabilities or performance. In many respects, the Panther was merely an enlarged MAN VK 24.01 with sloped armor and a bigger gun tacked on that was rushed into production and combat. MAN's engineers designed the chassis and running gear for a 24-ton tank but ended up carrying a 45-ton load, which severely strained the engine and transmission. While the "teething problems" of the Panther at Kursk are well known, less appreciated is the fact that these problems

SPECIFICATIONS: T-34

General
Production run: T-34/76: September 1940– March 1944
Model 1943: October 1943– March 1944
Vehicles produced: All T-34/76: 34,902
Model 1943: 10,760
Combat weight: 30.9 tons (metric)
Crew: four (tank commander, loader, driver mechanic, radio operator)

Dimensions
Overall length: 6.75m
Hull length: 6.09m
Width (with battle tracks): 3m
Height: 2.6m

Armour
Hull front: 47mm (at 30 degrees)
Hull sides: 60mm (at 50 degrees)
Hull rear: 47mm (at 45 degrees)
Hull roof: 20mm (at 0 degrees)
Turret front: 70mm (at 60 degrees)
Turret sides: 52mm (at 70 degrees)
Turret rear: 52mm (at 70 degrees)
Turret roof: 20mm (at 0 degrees)

Armament
Main gun: 1 x 76.2mm F-34 gun
Secondary: 2 x 7.62mm DT
Main gun rate of fire: 4–8rpm

Ammunition stowage
Main: 100 rounds (typically 75 OF-350 HE-Frag and 25 BR-350A APHE)
Secondary: 3,600 rounds

Communications
9R AM receiver/transmitter on 80% of tanks; intercom

Motive power
Engine: V-2 34 12-cylinder diesel engine
Power: 500hp at 1,800rpm
Fuel capacity: 610 liters
Power-to-weight ratio: 16.1hp/ton

Performance
Ground pressure: 0.83kg/cm^2
Maximum road speed: 55kph
Maximum cross-country speed: 40kph
Operational range (road): 432km
Operational range (cross-country): 57km
Fuel consumption (road): 1.41 liters/km
Fuel consumption (cross-country): 1.65 liters/km
Cost: 135,000 rubles

1. 76mm BR-350A (APHE)
2. 76mm OF-350 (HE-FRAG)

dogged the tank for the rest of 1943 and, indeed, its entire career. A report by Generaloberst Guderian's Panzer Commission in January 1945 reported that the final drives on 370 Panthers on the Eastern Front had failed and that the troops were losing confidence in "defective weapons." The Panther did enjoy a huge advantage in firepower over any other existing medium tank, but in terms of mobility, armored protection, and overall reliability, the Panther failed to either best the T-34/76 or to meet Guderian's initial requirements. In contrast, the T-34/76 was a mature design by 1943, with an optimum blend of armored protection and firepower. It was the T-34's superior mobility and reliability, combined with ease of production, that guaranteed a steady flow of replacement tanks that allowed the Red Army to seize and maintain the operational initiative in the Ukraine.

THE COMBATANTS

THE PANTHER TANK COMPANY

ORGANIZATION

A standard Heer (army) Panther tank platoon in 1943 consisted of five tanks and 25 soldiers, led by a platoon leader (either a Leutnant or Oberfeldwebel). The Panther companies in Panzer Battalions 51 and 52 that fought in *Zitadelle* each had 22 tanks and 172 soldiers, led by an Oberleutenant. There were two different Panther company organizations; one with four platoons and one with three platoons. A Panther tank battalion in 1943 was assigned between 71 and 96 tanks and up to 1,160 soldiers, led by a Hauptman or Major. A Panther tank battalion also included eight Panther tanks that belonged to the Headquarters Company, an armored pioneer platoon supported with halftracks, and towed antiaircraft guns. Compared to the Soviets, the Germans lavishly equipped their tank battalion with support assets: each tank company was supported by a J-Gruppe with six vehicles loaded with spare parts and capable of pulling an engine out. The key asset in each Panther battalion was the recovery section, which might have a couple of Bergepanthers or up to nine Zgkw 18-ton semitracks. These were the primary means of recovering damaged or inoperative Panthers. The Panther battalions also had a large supply platoon, with 47 heavy trucks capable of hauling ammunition or fuel. Although it was intended for Panther units to operate attached to existing Panzer divisions, during the chaotic summer of 1943 most Panther units operated semi-independently, and it was not unusual for companies to be temporarily attached to other commands.

THE GERMAN PANZER SOLDIER, 1943

Unlike their Soviet counterparts, German Panzer soldiers usually volunteered for the armor branch. Furthermore, most of the German Panzer soldiers were considerably older and more experienced than the Russian crews. Typical Panther tank platoon leaders were 26 to 30 years old, and company commanders were 27 to 31 years old. At least half the platoon leaders and noncommissioned officers (NCOs) had been in the Wehrmacht since 1938 or 1939 and had some combat experience, although oftentimes in the infantry or other branches. Typical Panther Unteroffiziers were 22 years old and already had three years of military experience under their belts. However, the German NCO corps by 1943 could no longer be so selective, and not all men promoted were up to a high caliber. The heart of each Panther company was the "Spieß" ("mother of the company") – a Hauptfeldwebel (first sergeant). While the average soldier in a Panther unit had an edge in experience over his Soviet counterpart, it is also important to note the negative impact of wounds and combat fatigue upon the surviving cadre of veterans after two continuous years of war in Russia.

TRAINING SCHOOLS

The Third Reich went to great effort to train its Panzertruppen as combat-ready "hunters," but as the war progressed, the training programs were shortened and resources such as fuel became increasingly scarce. The formation of the first Panther units coincided with the appointment of Generaloberst Guderian as Inspector of Panzer Troops in February 1943. Guderian took charge of an already good training system and streamlined it to produce tankers who were prepared for actual combat conditions. Unfortunately, the technical problems with the early Panther Ausf. D models severely distracted the troops of the 51st and 52nd Panzer Battalions, and units formed later received much better training.

Enlisted soldiers completed 16 weeks of basic infantry training before going to basic tank training at Panzerschule 1 in Wünsdorf for four more months. The Panzer school provided extremely thorough driver and basic maintenance training to enlisted soldiers as well as cross training on other crew functions. After completing the Panzer school, promising soldiers could be sent to either NCO or officer candidate training, which might require another six to nine months. Once all individual training was complete, new officers, NCOs, and enlisted troops were then assigned to a Panzer Ersatz Abteilung, a replacement tank battalion for each panzer division. Temporary crews and subunits were formed in the replacement battalions in order to conduct crew, platoon, and company training. While at the replacement battalion, selected crews or individuals would be sent to specialist schools such as the superb gunner's course at the Army Gunnery School at Putlos.

Guderian ordered that the primary focus on unit training should be the live-fire "battle run," and he instituted an abbreviated tank training program in May 1943 that put primary emphasis on gunnery. During the battle run, crews had to engage a series of moving and pop-up stationary targets, with both AP and high-explosive (HE) rounds, at ranges from 800 to 2,000m. Against stationary tanks, a Panther crew was expected to obtain at least one hit out of four rounds fired against a frontal tank target at 1,200 to 2,000m. Another sequence was to engage a target moving at 20kph on a sled at a range of 800 to 1,200 meters. The target had to be hit with one of three rounds and within 30 seconds. German target silhouettes in 1943 were 4m long and 2m high, which was smaller than an actual T-34. Guderian also mandated that that at least 30 percent of training should be conducted at night or under low-light conditions.

Once the order came from the OKH to begin forming the first Panther battalions, the decision was made to establish a Panther training course at Erlangen on March 1, 1943, near Grafenwöhr, where much of the Panther testing occurred. The Panther course included both an individual phase for training soldiers on the new features of

A Panther Ausf. A searching for targets during a movement to contact. German tank crews normally moved forward slowly, trying to spot Soviet antitank guns or dug-in T-34s before they opened fire. (Author's collection)

Panther 824 from the 52nd Panzer Battalion, knocked out during *Zitadelle* and captured on July 19, 1943. The nearly intact Panther was sent back to Chelyabinsk for technical evaluation. (Tank Museum, Bovington)

the tank as well as a collective phase for training platoons and companies. Generally, the Panther course was intended to last about two months, but because some battalions such as I/Panzer Regiment 1 did not go through it all at once, the process could be stretched out. Once the school was fully functional by May, it could produce one trained battalion per month, plus individual replacements. Panzer Battalion 51, based upon the II/Panzer Regiment 33 from 9th Panzer Division, began forming at Grafenwöhr on January 13, 1943, and Panzer Battalion 52 was formed from the 11th Panzer Division's I/Panzer Regiment 15 on February 6. Between January and June 1943, these battalions spent much of their time working with MAN engineers to identify and correct the numerous defects in the first batch of Panther Ausf. D tanks rather than engaging in collective training. A few Panther crews were sent to the Putlos gunnery school, but collective training above the platoon level never occurred at Erlangen. In April 1943, both battalions had to turn all their Panthers in for modifications, and since the troops now lacked tanks, a ridiculous decision was made to ship the troops to Mailly le Camp in France for "training." Unlike Soviet training camps in the Urals, the German Panzer crews were at risk of enemy air attack while in the rear areas. On April 17, four Panther crewmen from 2./Pz. Abt.51, including an experienced company commander and a platoon leader, were killed by an RAF bonbing raid on Mannheim when en route to France. The battalions were finally reassembled at Grafenwöhr in June, just in time to be reissued their tanks and to begin rail loading for the Eastern Front.

CREW AND UNIT FORMATION

Once the 51st and 52nd Panzer Battalions began forming at Grafenwöhr, the newly raised companies began assembling tank crews. Experienced tank commanders did have some choice regarding who was placed on their tank, although the company commander and platoon leaders usually received the better gunners and drivers.

Once formed, a crew would tend to stay together until casualties occurred. By the time that 1 Company of the 51st Panzer Battalion (1./Pz.Abt. 51) arrived by rail near Borisovka on July 1, it had grown to four officers and 190 enlisted men. Of the 194 troops in the company, 49 percent were veterans from Panzer Regiment 33, 43 percent were replacements, and 8 percent were from other units. The commander of the company was Oberleutnant Rudolf Köhler, an old hand who had served first as a tank platoon leader in Poland, Holland, France, and Greece, then as a company commander in southern Russia from 1941 to 1942. While the company had a solid core of experienced veterans, slightly more than half the troops had not previously seen combat.

Although the OKH had specified in June 1943 that all panzer divisions on the Eastern Front would receive one Panther battalion in the next six months, the decision was made to group the 51st and 52nd Panzer Battalions under the provisional 39th Panzer Regiment, led by Major Meinrad von Lauchert. Interestingly, von Lauchert had been in the 4th Panzer Division's Panzer Regiment 35 during the fighting around Mtensk against Katukov's T-34s in October 1941. Now he stood to lead Germany's answer to the T-34 in to its first battle.

CREW ROLES AND FUNCTIONS

The five-man crew of a Panther consisted of the Panzerführer (tank commander; usually a Leutnant, Feldwebel, or Unteroffizier), the Richtschutze (gun layer, or gunner ; usually an Unteroffizier or Obergefreiter), the Ladeschutze (loader; typically

Panther Ausf. D of the 39th Panzer Regiment rail-loaded at Grafenwöhr on June 24–28, 1943 and headed east to participate in Operation *Zitadelle*. It took six days for the Panthers to reach their unloading point at Borisovka. (Robert L Hunt Library)

MAJOR KARL VON SIVERS

Major Karl von Sivers (1912–1944), commander of the 52nd Panzer Battalion. Commissioned as a cavalry officer in 1934, von Sivers served in the 1st Cavalry Division in 1939–41. Von Sivers was a traditional horse cavalryman but he came from an educated background, speaking four languages including Russian. In December 1941, von Sivers' regiment began converting into the 2nd Battalion, 24th Panzer Regiment and he served in that unit during the advance to Stalingrad in 1942, but he managed to avoid the fate of most of his unit. On March 15, 1943, von Sivers took command of the 1st Battalion, Panzer Regiment 15, which was forming the 52nd Panzer Battalion. Although von Sivers helped to form the new battalion at Grafenwöhr, he was not able to deploy with the unit for Operation *Zitadelle* due to illness. He re-joined the 52nd Panzer Battalion near Tomarovka on July 22, 1943 and conducted a skillful withdrawal down the Vorskla River valley in the face of the Soviet onslaught in August 1943. Von Sivers remained in command of the battalion after it was re-designated as the 1st Battalion, Panzer Regiment 15 on August 24 until he was killed in action in March 1944. Von Sivers was typical of the mid-war German panzer leader, who was not a "tank ace" himself, but whose experienced leadership enabled the Panther units to hold together under extreme conditions.

Image courtesy of Jason Mark

OBERFELDWEBEL GERHARD BREHME

Oberfeldwebel Gerhard Brehme (1912–1943), platoon leader in 1st Company, Panzer Battalion 52. Brehme was typical of the German mid-war tank sergeant. He had served in the 1st Battalion, Panzer Regiment 15 since Operation *Barbarossa* began. On January 9, 1943, Brehme was a platoon leader in Group Wöhler, the effort to relieve the trapped German garrison at Velikiye Luki. Although the effort failed, Brehme was credited with destroying eight Soviet tanks during the operation. Brehme then was sent back to Grafenwöhr where he trained on the new Panther tank with the 52nd Panzer Battalion. However during Operation *Zitadelle*, Brehme was one of the first casualties. His Panther – probably Number 521 – was hit in the thin hull side armor by two 76mm armor-piercing rounds near Dubrova on July 6, 1943. Brehme was badly burned and he died in the military hospital in Kharkov on July 17, 1943. After *Zitadelle*, Brehme's Panther ended up on display in Gorky Park in Moscow. Brehme was an experienced tanker who was credited with destroying 51 enemy tanks during his career and it was this type of steadfast NCO who held the Wehrmacht together during the tough summer and fall of 1943.

Image: Bundesarchiv BILD183-R64504

an Obergefreiter or Gefreiter), the Funker (radio operator; a Gefreiter or Schütze), and the Fahrer (driver; an Obergefreiter or Gefreiter). By having a dedicated gunner, the Panther commander could concentrate on not only fighting his own tank but leading his section, platoon, or company. Unlike Soviet T-34 drivers, the Panther driver was trained to make independent decisions and to use terrain for concealment as much as possible. The Panther crew was trained to think and fight as a team with every member participating in combat. For example, the radio operator would spot for the gunner and pass him any corrections over the intercom. Since all five crewmembers were hooked into the tank's intercom system, the situational awareness and coordination between them was easier.

THE T-34 TANK COMPANY

ORGANIZATION

The T-34/76 tank platoon consisted of three tanks and 12 soldiers, usually led by a Leytenant Platoon Leader. It was therefore much smaller than a Panther company. In theory, each tank was supposed to be commanded by an officer, but in practice, two out of three tanks were commanded by a Serzhant (Sergeant). The tank company had three platoons totaling ten T-34/76 tanks and 42 soldiers, including the company commander, who in 1943 was typically a Starshiy Leytenant (Senior Lieutenant). A Soviet tank battalion in 1943 was authorized 31 T-34/76 tanks and about 180 soldiers and was led by a Kapetan or Major. The tank battalion also included a

During the training of the 51st and 52nd Panzer Battalions, their Panther tanks had to be rail-loaded and sent back to the factories for rebuilding in April 1943. Lacking tanks for over a month, the crews were forced to conduct simulated crew drills on foot. (Robert L Hunt Library)

small 11-man tank and weapons repair section, a transportation section with a truck for fuel, and several supply trucks for ammunition, and a four-man medical section. Some units had a "Zhuchka," a turretless T-34 equipped as a recovery vehicle, but many just had a GAZ-AA repair truck or captured German vehicles. Normally, the smallest Soviet armored unit given independent missions was a tank brigade, with two to three tank battalions.

THE SOVIET TANK SOLDIER, 1943

Soviet tank platoon leaders were usually 19 to 21 years old, while company commanders were 22 to 27 years old. Many junior officers had been members of the Communist Komsomol organization as teenagers and typically were high school graduates. Sergeants were usually 18 years old and might have been in the Red Army for six months, although there were a handful of surviving enlisted men from the 1942 fighting who were often made the company Starshina (Master Sergeant). Each tank platoon usually had a Starshiy Serzhant (Senior Sergeant) who acted as a platoon sergeant, or even as the platoon leader in case the Leytenant was a casualty. Petr Kirichenko, who served in the 159th Tank Brigade, was made a senior sergeant after only one month of training.[4]

Most young Soviet soldiers had been raised under conditions of poverty, limited education, and with poor diets compared to their German counterparts. According to platoon leader Evgeni Bessonov, "Most of the 18 year-old Soviet soldiers in 1943 were not physically strong, mostly small and frail youngsters."[5] Virtually to a man, the primary complaint for Soviet soldiers was the lack of food, a condition that was endemic in both the rear areas and at the front. Soviet battlefield logistics were so primitive that as tank units advanced through the Ukraine, soldiers relied on "grandmother's rations" – food from local civilians. However, alcohol was plentiful, and Soviet commanders were often very lenient about allowing troops to drink before battle in order to allay fears about heavy losses. Soviet tankers were under orders not to abandon their T-34s unless they were either burning or the main gun was disabled. To do otherwise was to risk being sent to a *shtrafbat* (punishment battalion). Thus, fear of harsh punishment by the People's Commissariat for Internal Affairs (NKVD) caused Soviet tankers to stick with their tanks to the end.

TRAINING SCHOOLS

The three main T-34 production centers in Nizhniy Tagil, Sverdlovsk, and Chelyabinsk all had colocated tank training regiments (TZAP). There were also tank schools at Kurgan, Ufa, Ulyanovsk, and Saratov that taught basic skills such as driving and familiarization with the V-2 diesel engine to both officer cadets and enlisted troops. By 1943, Soviet enlisted soldiers usually spent four to eight weeks receiving basic training in a tank training battalion. There were separate battalions for drivers, loaders, and

---

4   See Artem, Drabkin and Oleg Sheremet, *T-34 in Action*, Pen & Sword, Barnsley, UK, 2006, pp. 110–111.
5   See Bessonov, Evgeni, *Tank Rider: Into the Reich with the Red Army*, Casemate, Philadelphia, 2003, p. 44.

radiomen. Unlike German tank schools, Soviet tank drivers were generally not taught how to make use of battlefield terrain, nor were they taught to make independent decisions. Soviet schools considered a T-34 driver trained if he could start the vehicle and drive it in a column of other tanks or in a simple wedge, all conducted under noncombat conditions. Soldiers selected as loaders spent endless hours practicing loading dummy rounds into a breach and loading machine gun drums. Radio operators were given only the basics: how to turn on the receiver/transmitter (R/T) and how to change frequencies. Cross training of crewmembers was rare, and usually only the designated driver was capable of driving the tank.

After initial basic training was judged completed, the more promising trainees were sent to either NCO or officer candidate training. Some candidates may also have been sent to other technical schools in order to be trained as tank mechanics. Even in 1943, much of the tank training was conducted on worn-out BT-7 or T-26 tanks, with only a few T-34s available for training. Soviet training units in rear areas often wasted their trainees' limited time with pointless drills, the memorizing of field manuals, and endless political lectures. Training under simulated combat conditions was negligible. Leytenant Bessonov, of the 49th Mechanized Brigade in 1943, said that, "The level of training was poor, as the teachers did not understand the subject themselves" and some martinets still managed to include "ceremonial march step" in the officer training syllabus in 1942.[6] Leytenant Pavlov V. Bryukhov, who trained at the Kurgan Tank Training School from January to April 1943, said that "Training at the base was very

A decorated T-34 crew. Note the commander's cupola on the T-34/76 Model 1943 and the female crew member. By the middle of 1943 women tank drivers were beginning to appear in some Guards units, but they were relatively few in number. (Courtesy of the Central Museum of the Armed Forces Moscow)

6   See Bessonov, p. 28.

weak" and the tank gunnery ranges lacked the kind of pop-up or moving targets that he observed on tank ranges in Germany after the war. Bryukhov said that most training consisted of driving on old BT tanks with new leytenants conducting only a single exercise dubbed "tank platoon in the offensive."[7] An even more telling indictment of Soviet tank training is that many platoon leaders could not even read a map, which became a frequent problem during the advance to the Dnepr River.

Once a soldier finished his basic training, he was usually sent to one of the tank training regiments located near a T-34 production center to receive his tank. The training regiments could typically process about 2,000 soldiers at a time. In theory, the soldier would spend only about one month at the tank training regiment, but in some cases, soldiers might stay there for a year or longer. The tank factories were perennially short of labor, and tankers awaiting their tanks were often put to work on the assembly lines. When Leytenant Bryukhov completed training at Kurgan, he was sent to the 6th Tank Training Regiment at Chelyabinsk, but instead of receiving a T-34 tank, Bryukhov was put to work on a machine lathe in the Chelyabinsk tank plant for two weeks. The training regiments usually conducted simple platoon and company-level training such as practicing moving in a wedge or line, but there was little tactical training.

Actual crew training in Soviet tank units was incredibly brief. After the new T-34/76 was received at the factory, a group of about ten tanks would be assembled into a "march company" under the Senior Leytenant and then conducted a road march to a local gunnery range. According to several Soviet T-34 platoon leaders, familiarization firing in 1943 typically consisted of firing only three 76.2mm rounds and one drum of machine gun ammunition at static targets. Even if a newly formed crew performed miserably at this seemingly simple task, the tank was judged combat ready and ordered to move to a nearby railhead for shipment to the front. Some crew members were still not comfortable around tanks: Junior Leytenant Sergei Burtsev noted that his loader was so frightened by the recoil from the first round

A company of T-34/76 Model 1942 tanks advance on line. Oftentimes, crews were so poorly trained that only such simplistic tactics were possible. (From the fonds of the RGAKFD in Krasnogorsk)

7   See Drabkin, pp. 128–129.

LEYTENANT PAVLOVICH VASILY BRYUKHOV

Leytenant Pavlovich Vasiliy Bryukhov (1924–), T-34 platoon leader in 99th Tank Brigade, July 1943. Bryukhov was born in the Urals and had just completed high school at the start of the German invasion. Initially, Bryukhov served in a ski battalion in the defense of Kalinin in November 1941 where he was wounded. After recovering, Bryukhov was sent to Kurgan in September 1942 to receive initial tanker training and he was commissioned a junior lieutenant in April 1943. He joined up with his first crew at Chelyabinsk in May 1943. Bryukhov arrived at the 2nd Tank Corps just prior to the battle of Kursk and he fought as a T-34 platoon leader in the Ukraine for the rest of 1943. Bryukhov would eventually destroy a Panther tank at pointblank range in early 1944 and rose to battalion commander by the end of 1944 (at the age of 20). During 1943–45 Bryukhov was involved in numerous tank battles and had nine T-34s destroyed under him. Bryukhov was eventually made Hero of the Soviet Union and he claimed to have destroyed 28 German tanks.

SOVIET FEMALE TANKERS

Approximately one million women served in the Red Army in 1941–45, but fewer than 10 percent served in combat roles. A few female volunteers served as tank drivers early in 1942, but it was not until women were sent to serve as cadres in tank training regiments in January 1943 that their presence became more widespread. By the summer of 1943 the pool of Soviet manpower was beginning to run dry and a number of women who had served in the training units were sent as individual replacements, usually to Guards tank brigades. While the total number of female T-34 tank crew members is unknown, it was not large, although Communist propaganda tended to focus on these individuals. A few women that survived their initial combat rose to become tank commanders, but most served innocuously as drivers, who tended to have a low survival rate in combat. In one action near Fastov on November 8, 1943, SS Leibstandarte engaged two T-34s from the 3 GTA and discovered afterwards that both tanks had female crew members. Mariya Oktyabrskaya was the first female tank driver to become a Heroine of the Soviet Union, the most prestigious award for bravery. A widow of a soldier killed defending the Motherland, she sold all her possessions to raise the money to donate a tank to the military. Her only stipulation was that she would be its driver. She was posted to the 26th Guards Tank Brigade in September 1943 and saw repeated action

throughout the Eastern Front, in particular serving courageously in the fighting around the Vitebsk region in November 1943. Sr/Sgt Mariya Oktyabrskaya was eventually mortally wounded in combat in March 1944.

fired on the range that he jumped out of the T-34 and ran off. Once the march company arrived at a railhead near the combat zone, it often had to move considerable distances by track to link up with the battalion it had been assigned to. As the Germans retreated to the Dnepr River, it became vital for the Soviets to sustain their forward tank units by regular infusions of new tanks and crews. Even when a company arrived at the front and was integrated into a tank battalion there was usually little time for training. Just prior to Kursk, many Soviet tankers were sent to assist getting the local harvest in – so dire was the Red Army's food shortage – rather than conducting gunnery or maneuver training.

Despite the shortcomings in Soviet tactical training taught at the schools, frontline units were gradually learning how to counter German tanks. Unlike the battles in 1941–42, in which one inexperienced Soviet tank unit after another was annihilated, more Soviet tankers survived the winter battles of 1942–43 and provided a cadre of experienced tank crews who would make a big difference at Kursk and later engagements. In particular, the creation of Guards units pooled veteran tankers and experienced commanders, helping to bridge the gap between the Wehrmacht's qualitative approach to tank warfare and the Red Army's quantitative approach.

CREW FORMATION AND MARCH COMPANIES

Once an officer, NCO, or enlisted soldier arrived at the tank training regiment, the process of starting to form companies, platoons, and individual tank crews began. In addition to replacements, the training regiment was also a repository for wounded soldiers returning to duty, soldiers reassigned from other branches, and for survivors of tank units that had been shattered in combat. Leytenant Burtsev recalled that none

A platoon of late-model T-34/76 Model 1943 with commander's cupola. The introduction of this cupola corrected a design flaw and finally gave tank commanders the ability to fully view the battlefield. (Courtesy of the Central Museum of the Armed Forces Moscow)

of his four-man crew had any combat experience when they formed up at the Nizhniy Tagil Tank Plant and that the Red Army was beginning to scrape the bottom of the manpower barrel after Kursk. Burstev's driver was a malcontent with a long criminal record, his radio operator/gunner was a former restaurant waiter, and his loader was "a mental defective." Once at the front, the Soviets made little effort to keep crews together: Leytenant Bryukhov had ten different crews from 1943 to 1945.

CREW ROLES AND FUNCTIONS

The four-man crew of the T-34/76 consisted of the Komandir tanka (KT; tank commander), the Zatyajaletel (loader), the Mekhanik-voditel (MV; driver mechanic), and the Radist pulemetchik (RP; radio operator/machine gunner). As with the French Char B and Somua 35 tanks, the commander in the T-34/76 tank was expected to both direct his own tank – plus others if he was a platoon leader or company commander – and to aim and fire the main gun. This lack of a dedicated gunner in the T-34/76 seriously slowed down the process of target acquisition and over-burdened small unit leaders with too many tasks to perform. Soviet T-34/76 drivers were also ostensibly mechanics and responsible for the vehicle's maintenance needs, but in practice, the drivers mostly remained in their "holes" and drove the vehicle where they were told. The loader on the T-34/76 was also supposed to function as an observer and to fire the coaxial machine gun, but most loaders tended to view themselves as "passengers" and assumed a rather passive role unless kept under tight rein by the tank commander. The RP on the T-34/76 was fairly useless since at least one-third of tanks still lacked radios in the summer of 1943 and the hull machine gun was difficult to use. His main function was to help the driver shift gears while moving and to help with vehicle maintenance.

A T-34 crew "punches the gun tube" in order to clean the F-34's gun barrel of carbon residue after firing a significant number of rounds. (Tank Museum, Bovington)

49

COMBAT

KURSK, JULY 5–14

The Panthers of the 39th Panzer Regiment reached the Grossdeutschland Division's assembly area north of Moshchenoye late on July 4. Ominously, two Panthers were destroyed by engine fires on the short road march from the railhead, and 18 others broke down. Grossdeutschland began its own attack at 0400 hours on July 5, but the late-arriving Panthers were not in the first echelon, giving commander Major von Lauchert a few more hours to finish fueling and attempting to establish functioning radio nets.

At 0815 hours, von Lauchert began moving his two battalions with about 184 Panthers northward out of the assembly area and over the rail line northwest of Tomarovka. At least four Panthers caught fire from fuel leaks shortly after leaving the assembly area. On each remaining Panther, loaders slammed a Panzergranate 39/42 AP round into the breech for "battle carry" while gunners zeroed their sights to 1,000m. The regiment moved with Hauptman Heinrich Meyer's 51st Battalion in the lead, followed by the 52nd Panzer Battalion under the command of Major Gerhard Tebbe with its four companies in double row formation. The entire Panther regiment covered an area about 500m wide and almost 3km long. Smoke from burning corn set afire by artillery hung over the battlefield, limiting visibility. Grossdeutschland's advance guard was supposed to breach the first Soviet obstacle belt, and then the Panthers would exploit through the gap. However, this plan quickly fell apart. When the lead Panthers reached the 80m-wide Berezovyi Ravine, they found barbed wire obstacles, as well as mines, strewn over marshy area that was made virtually impassable by heavy rains the previous night.

Like most untried armor units, the 39th Panzer Regiment came to a virtual halt upon encountering the unexpected obstacle and began to bunch up. Grossdeutschland's pioneers had already assessed the initial crossing site as unsuitable for tanks and were looking for alternate crossing sites when the Panthers arrived. After a few minutes of confusion, either von Lauchert or Meyer decided to cross the ravine. Several Panthers from both the 1st and 2nd Companies attempted to cross through the narrow, cleared lane, but all of them quickly bogged down in the thick mud at the bottom of the ravine, and their weak final drives could not get them up the opposite slope. Seeing this pile-up, Oberleutnant Helmut Langhammer tried to maneuver his trailing 4th Company westward to cross at a different spot. However, he quickly ran into an uncleared minefield and was wounded when his tank was disabled. The Soviet TM-41 AT mine, with four kilograms of Amatol, could break the track on a Panther and damage the road wheel arms. In short order, about 25 Panthers from the 51st Panzer Battalion and Regimental Stab were immobilized in the ravine due to the combination of mud, mines, and breakdowns. Furthermore, the weak final drive on the Panther Ausf. D could not easily reverse on muddy slopes, and the tanks began sheering teeth from their drive sprockets and overheating in a futile attempt to escape. Soviet artillery began pounding the huge, immobilized mass of German armor in their "kill zone." Although the Panther's armor was generally impervious to this barrage, Langhammer's Panther 401 was destroyed by a lucky ricochet into its belly armor, many other tanks suffered moderate damage and at least six crewmen were killed.

The advance guard from the Grossdeutschland Division found a better crossing site 1.5km to the west, and by early afternoon their pioneers established two narrow breaches. Von Lauchert shifted his regiment to the new site, and by 0400, about 30 Panthers, 15 Pz IVs, and four infantry battalions were across. The main Soviet defense in this area was centered upon the town of Cherkasskoye, held by the 196th Guards Rifle Regiment and two AT regiments. As dusk approached, the

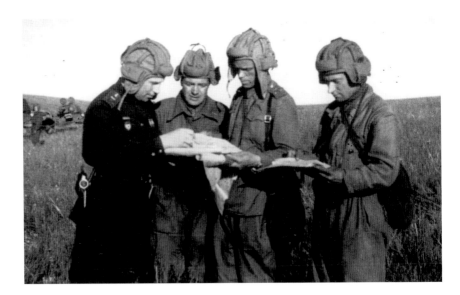

Grossdeutschland's infantry and assault guns broke into the town. Von Lauchert's Panthers assisted mopping up the village and thwarting a Soviet counterattack.

The Panthers had accomplished very little on their first day of combat yet had suffered heavy losses from tactical ineptitude and mechanical unreliability. By the morning of July 6, von Lauchert had only 50 to 80 Panthers operational in Yarki, although recovery was continuing in the Berezovyi Ravine. The commander of the 48th Panzer Corps decided to reorient the German attack toward the northeast, in part to avoid the thick Soviet defenses along the Pena River and also to avoid a repetition of the Berezovyi disaster. Grossdeutschland's Panzer regiment kicked off the attack at 1040 hours, with its tanks on the right side of the road toward Dubrova and the Panthers supposedly on the left side. However, von Lauchert was too busy trying to reorganize his disrupted regiment and failed to move out on schedule, while 10th Tank Brigade commander, Oberst Decker, failed to coordinate with the Grossdeutschland's panzers. Consequently, the Panther regiment blundered forward with little idea where friend or foe was located.

Meanwhile, in the low ground near Alekseyevka on the south side of the Pena River, there were three companies of dug-in T-34 tanks from the 14th Tank Regiment (3rd Mechanized Corps) deployed to reinforce the second defensive belt. The T-34s were well camouflaged and their hulls dug-in, presenting very small targets. Despite the lack of formal tactical training, veteran Soviet tankers had learned from bitter experience how to use terrain to counteract superior German gunnery. The T-34s covered an AT ditch and minefield to their south, backed up by three battalions of motorized infantry and AT guns. To the southeast, the 16th Tank Regiment and the rest of the 3rd Mechanized Brigade covered the other side of the AT ditch and minefield. The Soviet defense formed an L-shaped ambush as the Germans approached across flat, grassy terrain and cornfields. Grossdeutschland's advance guard came under direct, heavy fire, and the regimental commander, Oberst Graf von Strachwitz, was incensed about the lack of support from the Panthers.

Von Lauchert's Panthers were lost, inching forward through unfamiliar terrain, still uncertain where their objective lay. The regiment was deployed mostly in double columns with only the lead company in a wedge. Without infantry support, the Panthers never spotted the obstacle or enemy infantry and tanks until they bumped into the first mines 2km east of Cherkasskoye. Several tanks were immediately immobilized. Major Gerhard Tebbe's battalion was in the lead, and he froze in the kill zone. Soviet artillery began to pound the stalled cluster of Germans. In the first Panther versus T-34 duels of the war, the T-34s from the 14th Tank Regiment began to engage the clustered Panther column with flank shots from about 1,000–1,200m. Although Soviet gunnery was not particularly good, the Panthers were not moving much and were presenting their thin side armor to the enemy. Oberfeldwebel Gerhard Brehme, a platoon leader in the 5th Company of the 52nd Panzer Battalion, apparently became one of the first Panthers to fall victim to a T-34 when his tank was hit with a 76mm AP round that punched into his left side armor and ignited one of the fuel cells. Brehme managed to bail out of his burning Panther but was so badly burned that he died 12 days later. Major Tebbe lost control, and the veteran 8th Company commander, Oberleutnant Erdmann Gabriel, took charge, attempting to maneuver out of the zone.

Gabriel ordered his Panthers to engage the well-hidden T-34s, and some of the veteran German gunners hit a few of their elusive foes. The long hours invested in gunnery training on the ranges at Putlos and Grafenwöhr now proved its worth. Soviet tank commanders were surprised by the effectiveness of the new 75mm guns, and some T-34 platoons began to reposition to avoid the heaviest fire. Several T-34s were destroyed while pulling out of their hull-down positions – betrayed by their telltale grimy exhaust – thus becoming the first victims of the Panther's KwK 42 gun. Shortly, Soviet direct fire slackened, and von Lauchert was able to extract the surviving Panthers from this ambush and head southeast in the tracks of Grossdeutschland.

The large driver's hatch on the T-34 made ammunition loading easier and offered better chances for escape in the event of the tank being hit. (Courtesy of the Central Museum of the Armed Forces Moscow)

Von Lauchert's Panthers caught up with Grossdeutschland's tanks shortly after the main AT ditch was breached, and an angry von Strachwitz ordered the Panther unit to take the lead. Upon crossing the ditch, the Panthers moved off in the general direction of Dubrova, but some tanks became disoriented in the dust and smoke that surrounded the breach site. Eventually, the remnants of von Lauchert's battered regiment and Kampfgruppe von Strachwitz reached a hill on the outskirts of Dubrova and settled into a defensive lager for the night. July 6 had been another bad day for the 39th Panzer Regiment with 19 Panthers knocked out or destroyed compared to the destruction of no more than ten or 12 T-34s. Major Tebbe was quietly replaced by Hauptman Georg Baumunk, a combat-experienced officer from the disbanded 22nd Panzer Division. With the brigade's command and control totally disrupted after less than 48 hours of combat, Oberst Decker decided to leave this mess, and the remaining Panthers were put under von Strachwitz's command.

July 7 was a hot, hazy day. By dawn, Major von Lauchert had only 50 operational Panthers remaining under his command. At 0845 hours, von Strachwitz ordered the attack into the Soviet second defensive belt to continue, with the objective being to seize Dubrova and then move north to envelop the Soviet defenses at Syrtsev. Kampfgruppe von Strachwitz attacked with about 50 Panthers and 30 Pz III/IV. Most of the Soviet defenders had pulled out of Dubrova during the night, but the 3rd Mechanized Corps had established excellent defensive positions around Syrtsev, with about 20 dug-in T-34s from the 16th Tank Regiment and a few 85mm AT guns from the 756th Antitank Battalion. The Soviet defenders saw the approaching German

PANTHER GUNNER'S VIEW, AUGUST 1943

Commander: *Panzergranate! Laden und sichern!* Load Armor Piercing!
Loader: *Panzergranate geladen!* Armor Piercing loaded

Commander: *3 Uhr! Panzergranate – 800 – Panzer!* 3 o' clock! Armor piercing – 800m – tank!
Gunner: *Achtung!* On the way!

armor but did not open up with their antitank weapons until the Panzers ran into a minefield in a ravine just east of Syrtsev. Once again, the Panthers presented their vulnerable side armor to the Soviet gunners, and in minutes, about 15 Panthers were hit and set afire by 76mm and 85mm AP shells.

The Soviet gunners held a higher position than the Panthers who were stuck in the ravine, allowing them to hit the thinner armor on the turret roof. Soviet T-34 commanders fired as rapidly as possible, and their loaders, who were not issued asbestos gloves as were the German tankers, scorched their hands as they labored to throw red-hot spent shell casings out of the turret. Lieutenant Vasiliy Bryukhov, a T-34 platoon leader in the nearby 2nd Tank Corps, described engaging German tanks during *Zitadelle*:

> I'd get a target in the gun sight – a short stop, one shot, another one. I'd traverse the gun from left to right and shout: "Armor-piercing! Fragmentation!" The engine would be roaring so one couldn't hear the explosions outside, and when I opened fire myself I didn't hear anything that was happening outside the tank. Only when the tank was hit by an armor-piercing round . . . would I realize that there were also some guys firing at me."[8]

The situation was no easier for German tank crews. Oberleutnant Gabriel, in Panther 801, tried to assault through the ambush but did not get very far. Gabriel later wrote:

---

8   See Drabkin, p. 130.

A Panther platoon is crossing the line of departure in *keil* or "arrow" formation. Doctrine is to "battle carry" armor piercing Panzergranate 39/42 rounds, with battle sight set at 1,000m. The Panther advances with cupola hatch open, commander scanning forward with binoculars. The platoon commander has assigned each tank a specific area and this tank's gunner periodically traverses the turret about 30 degrees left to right to scan his zone with his TFZ 12 sight. The commander spots a stationary T-34/76 tank in defilade about 800m to his right flank. The tell-tale grimy exhaust gives away the T-34's position. Even before he speaks, he taps the gunner's right shoulder with his boot in order to alert him.

The driver brings the vehicle to a smooth halt to stabilize the firing platform. The gunner uses his foot pedal to traverse so that the center triangle of the left reticule is on the T-34's turret ring and uses 5x magnification. He fires the main gun with his center foot pedal. The brief flash and smoke

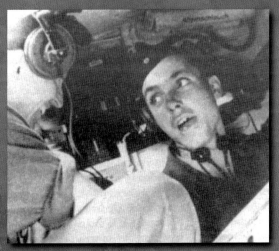

German tank gunner's position, with commander right behind him. An illustration of the cramped quarters within the tank.

rising from the T-34 turret shows that the target has been destroyed.

55

I was severely hit by an anti-tank round that penetrated the munitions chamber at the left side causing the later to explode immediately . . . I tore off the smoldering headset and microphone with my severely burnt hands, which already had the fingernails popped off. By then the gunner was pushing out from below, but I had to push his head so as to get out of the turret myself. This all happened very fast . . . After me, the gunner was still able to rescue himself. He had suffered burns, mainly on his face.

Despite heavy casualties, von Lauchert, Baumunk, and Meyer were able to get some of their Panthers to lay down suppressive fire against the dug-in T-34s and AT guns while a few tanks and infantrymen struggled to get through the obstacle. The veteran NCO tank gunners in the Panthers put the KwK 42 to good use by engaging T-34s over 1,000m away. Although the T-34s were virtually immune to fire in their hull-down positions, the Panther gunners merely waited until they rose up to fire and then rapidly pumped several rounds into their turrets. Gradually, the Panther gunners gained the upper hand, and the Kampfgruppe was finally able to cross the ravine and push north of Syrtsev. After overrunning some of the dug-in T-34s and infantry positions, about 20 Panthers were able to reach the vicinity of Gremuchy by dusk. It had been a disastrous day for the Panther regiment with 27 Panthers knocked out or destroyed. Von Strachwitz claimed that his Kampfgruppe destroyed 62 enemy tanks – about 35 to 40 by the Panthers – and the Soviet 3rd Mechanized Brigade had lost almost all its T-34s. Although the Panther had demonstrated its superior gunnery over the T-34, the heavy losses seriously affected morale in the regiment. Walter Rahn from the 52nd Panzer Battalion noted, "We felt the day was a defeat and long thereafter referred to the "Panther cemetery at Dubrova."

Over the next four days, the remnants of the Panther regiment attempted to exploit the small gap created in the Soviet second defensive belt, engaging in much heavy fighting around the village of Verkhopen'ye. Kampfgruppe von Strachwitz had about ten to 20 Panthers, a handful of Tigers, and about 25 Pz III/IV at this time, opposing the fresh 112th and 200th Tank Brigades from the 6th Tank Corps. Katukov, the 1st Tank Army commander, committed the 6th Tank Corps to stem the German breach in his lines, and the Panther and T-34 met in a series of small-scale meeting engagements. Some 13 Panthers were knocked out or destroyed in these four days, and many more broke down from increasingly serious mechanical defects. Both Soviet tank brigades were badly hurt in these battles, suffering about 60 percent losses, and the Germans were left in possession of a small salient around Verkhopen'ye. By July 12, the 39th Panzer Regiment was combat ineffective from losses and virtually out of ammunition, and it was pulled out of the line for resupply and reconstitution. A total of 31 Panthers had been destroyed in the first week in combat and 148 were under repair, leaving only 25 operational. The very high number of mechanical breakdowns indicated that Guderian had been correct: the Panther was not ready for combat.

The Panther regiment fought its last action on July 14 when 36 Panthers participated in a counterattack to repulse an attack by the 1st Tank Army's 86th Tank Brigade near Verkhopen'ye. For the first time, the Panther fought on the defensive, and it was now the T-34s who were moving across open terrain. The Panthers and a company of Pz IVs destroyed 28 T-34s at a cost of six Panthers and three Pz IVs. The next day, Operation *Zitadelle* was cancelled and von Lauchert began assembling his remaining Panthers to withdraw to Tomarovka. The German armor had not broken through to Kursk, and the Panthers had not proven decisive, or even mechanically reliable.

Von Lauchert and Decker claimed that the Panthers destroyed 263 enemy tanks during the period July 5 to 14. They also made absurd claims that Panthers routinely destroyed T-34s at 1,500–2,000m and even destroyed a T-34 at 3,000m. These claims are suspect and were probably made to overshadow the poor performance of the regiment during *Zitadelle*. Most of the Panther versus T-34 engagements in the first week of *Zitadelle* were against camouflaged, dug-in Soviet tanks, which made long-range engagements unlikely. In fact, most Panther versus T-34 engagements in this period were in the range of 800–1,200m, and Soviet records indicate that only a

A platoon of late-model T-34/76 Model 1943 tanks advancing with desant troops. The fact that T-34s advanced with their own infantry gave them a tactical advantage, allowing them to operate in villages and wooded areas with some degree of security. (From the fonds of the RGAKFD in Krasnogorsk)

handful of T-34s were destroyed at ranges above 1,500m. Furthermore, the large numbers of Panthers knocked out indicates that Soviet T-34s were engaging them from 1,200m or less, the maximum at which flank shots were likely to be effective. Given the fact that the regiment was ambushed three times in the first three days and had only a company or two operational for the rest of *Zitadelle*, the claim that the Panthers destroyed more than half the enemy tanks destroyed by the 48th Panzer Corps is absurd. The total number of enemy tanks knocked out or destroyed by the Panthers was probably about 120, of which fewer than 100 were T-34s. On July 20, the 39th Panzer Regiment reported that it had 41 operational Panthers, 85 under repair, and 58 total losses, of which 49 were blown up by the Germans themselves. Although Hitler had ordered that no Panthers were to fall into Soviet hands, seven knocked-out Panthers were captured on July 19. The first round of the duel between Panthers and T-34s had clearly gone to the Soviet tankers, who, while bloodied, had prevented a German breakthrough, and were still capable of offensive operations.

AKHTYRKA AND KHARKOV, AUGUST 3–26

Between July 17 and 19, the 39th Panzer Regiment moved back to Tomarovka and was disbanded. The 51st Panzer Battalion handed over its remaining Panthers to the 52nd Battalion, and its personnel proceeded by rail to Bryansk, where they received 96 factory-fresh Panthers. The 52nd Panzer Battalion, with Major von Sivers back in command, was attached to the 19th Panzer Division and concentrated on repairing its damaged Panthers. In one of the great tactical surprises of the war, the Voronezh front launched Operation *Rumantsyev*, the counteroffensive against the Belgorod salient, at 0500 hours on August 3. Vatutin concentrated the 1st Tank Army (1TA) and 5th Guards Tank Army (5GTA) with about 800 T-34s on a narrow

Given the superb mobility of the T-34, Soviet armor units were able to advance rapidly to the Dnepr, upsetting German plans to defend behind the river. Throughout 1943, the Soviet ability to shift tank corps 200 kilometers or more in a couple of days and then attack shocked the Germans.

12km front between Tomarovka and Belgorod. By the end of the first day, the 5GTA had penetrated 26km into the German defenses. The Soviet offensive caught von Sivers with only 27 operational Panthers and 109 under repair. Since most of his tanks were immobile, von Sivers was ordered to organize a defensive hedgehog around Tomarovka and prepare for local counterattacks. By August 4, the Soviet 6th Tank Corps had already pushed south of Tomarovka and was threatening to cut off the 52nd Panzer Battalion and the 19th Panzer Division. Von Sivers's Panthers destroyed seven T-34s from the 200th Tank Brigade outside Tomarovka, but on August 5, he decided on to retreat down the Vorskla River valley toward the repair depot in Borisovka.

After blowing up 72 immobilized Panthers, von Sivers's Kampfgruppe began retreating southwest with a mixed assortment of about 2,000 German troops. Although this "floating pocket" was virtually surrounded by the Soviet 1TA, the Panther's long-range gunnery was able to keep Soviet armor at a distance. Late on August 6, the Soviet 31st Tank Corps tried to cut off the column south of Borisovka, but the Panthers destroyed 17 T-34s at no cost to themselves. By August 8, von Sivers's group had reached Grayvoron, where the Soviet 5th Guards Tank Corps had already encircled the town. On the afternoon of August 8, a company-size probe from the 13th Guards Tank Brigade found von Sivers's Kampfgruppe. Walter Rahn wrote, "Early in the afternoon, armor-piercing shells hit our position. A few minutes later, 12 enemy tanks with mounted infantry attacked our all-round defensive positions. After eight T-34s had been put out of action, the remaining Russian tanks withdrew."[9] However, von Sivers's Panthers were virtually out of fuel and were only kept moving thanks to Luftwaffe aerial resupply. On August 9, von Sivers's Kampfgruppe linked up with the Grossdeutschland Division near Akhtyrka, which had broken out from Soviet encirclement, destroying 40 T-34s in the process for no combat loss to themselves. However, 16 out of 27 Panthers broke down on the 100km march and only nine were operational once they reached Akhtyrka.

---

9   See Rahn, Walter, "Fighting Withdrawal of Kampfgruppe Von Sivers . . ." an unpublished paper by
    the former orderly of Panzer Battalion 52.

A Panther from the 1st Panzer Division engaging a T-34 in November 1943. This is one of the very few images in existence showing a real Panther vs T-34 engagement.

The 51st Panzer Battalion returned to the 4th Panzer Army in early August and was attached to Grossdeutschland at Akhtyrka, but it was committed into combat piecemeal as it arrived by rail. On the morning of August 9, a Kampfgruppe of seven Panthers from the 4./Pz. 51 and four Tigers under the command of Hauptman Kikibusch attacked to clear away elements of the Soviet 10th Tank Corps from the rail station at Trostyanets north of Akhtyrka. While moving out of the assembly area, a Panther's engine caught fire and the tank burned out. Unteroffizier Peter Schamberger, the gunner on Panther 442, described the movement:

> Our tubes point forward and to the flanks, we advance nervously, watching the trail . . .
> Two hundred meters after leaving the woods, we make a short halt. Suddenly, anti-tank
> weapons start shooting at us from a higher elevation. We react immediately and radio our
> position to the tanks remaining on the edge of the woods. Before we can receive new
> orders, our Panther receives some hits and we take shelter in . . . Very quickly, we leave in
> a group toward the village of Trostyanets, 7 kilometers away . . . Suddenly, a large number
> of tanks emerge in front of us. "Halte!": we hear on the radio. "Fire on the left!" The action
> is short and violent. Some T-34s begin to burn. We are favored compared to the T-34
> because our Panther has thicker armor and our 75mm guns are surprisingly precise.[10]

By the time the small German Kampfgruppe reached the outskirts of Trostyanets it was surrounded by Soviet tanks and AT guns and had to fight its way back to friendly lines. However, only a single Panther made it. Two Tigers and six Panthers were lost against a Soviet loss of three to five T-34s. This company-size action is illustrative of how the lack of reconnaissance, infantry support, and artillery seriously undermined the performance of Panthers and Tigers, which had to fight T-34s that were operating as part of a combined arms team. While the T-34 may have had inferior armor and firepower to the Panther and Tiger, the presence of infantry, AT guns, and plentiful

---

10 See Schamberger, Peter, "Le Bataillon de Panther de la 9.Pz.Div. en Russie ou l'historique de la Pz.Abt. 51 (2e partie) by Didier Lodieu, 39/45 *Magazine*, No. 187, February 2002, pp. 16–19.

artillery more than made up the difference. Thus, the idea of "pure" tank duels just did not fit the reality of the Eastern Front in mid-1943.

Grossdeutschland and the 51st Panzer Battalion arrived in Akhtyrka just ahead of Major General Pavel Poluboyarov's 4th Guards Tank Corps (4GTC), which made rapid progress down the east side of the Vorskla River valley. Poluboyarov tried to attack directly into the city with his 12th and 14th Guards Tank Brigades on August 10 and 11 but was repulsed. The 51st Panzer Battalion claimed 16 T-34s destroyed in these actions but lost 11 Panthers. Barred from direct entry into Akhtyrka, Poluboyarov attempted to envelop Akhtyrka from the south with his 13th Guards Tank Brigade (13GTB) while maintaining pressure from the east. Scraping together about 15 Panthers and ten Tigers, Grossdeutschland Division succeeded in stopping the 13GTB. By holding Akhtyrka, Grossdeutschland threatened the flank of Katukov's 1st Tank Army around Kotelva. The Germans decided to try and cut off the Soviet spearhead. On August 18, Grossdeutschland mounted a major counterattack into the 1st Tank Army's right flank in the hope of linking up with the SS-Totenkopf division's counterattack from the east. The attack was a complete success and was able to isolate both the 4th and 5th Guards Tank Corps around Kotelva. However, the attack was costly for the 51st Panzer Battalion. Hauptman Meyer was killed in action on August 19, and the battalion lost another 15 Panthers over the next week. Although the German counterattack succeeded in isolating Katukov's spearhead, the 4th Panzer Army could not hold its positions and was forced to yield Akhtyrka on August 24. The 51st Panzer Battalion claimed to have destroyed about 100 enemy tanks in August, but it was reduced to only 15 operational Panthers and had lost 53.

While Grossdeutschland was trying to keep Katukov's 1st Tank Army out of Akhtyrka, the 3rd Panzer Corps was fighting desperately to keep Rotmistrov's 5th Guards Tank Army out of Kharkov. The SS-Das Reich and Wiking Divisions returned from the Mius front, but they could only delay the inevitable as overwhelming Soviet force gradually wore down the defense. In the final act of the battle of Kharkov, the Das Reich's Panther battalion, the I/SS Panzer 2, arrived just as the city was about to fall. SS-Hauptsturmführer Hans Weiss arrived with two companies of Panthers and

A T-34/76 tank company in the attack. Unlike the Germans, the Soviets usually did not use "overwatch" tactics, using one element to cover the movement of another. (Courtesy of the Central Museum of the Armed Forces Moscow)

was immediately ordered to counterattack a Soviet breakthrough near Korotich and Lyubotin, southwest of Kharkov. The Soviet 24th Guards Tank Brigade under Lieutenant-Colonel V. P. Karpov had 110 T-34s but lost 53 in a three-hour battle with the Panthers. Junior Lieutenant Yuri M. Polyanovski, a platoon leader in the 24th Guards Tank Brigade, described what happened when his platoon tried to cross a railway embankment near Korotich:

> As soon as our tank tried to drive through the crossing – bang, it was finished. My tank became just another victim... Smoke filled the crew compartment, the tank halted and we had to bail out ...[11]

Lieutenant Vasiliy Bryukhov, also a platoon leader in the 5GTA, described his platoon's attack:

> We were about 200 meters from the enemy when the Germans hit my tank head-on with an armor-piercing round. The tank stopped but didn't catch fire. . . the round had penetrated our front armor by the radio operator's seat, killing him with splinters . . . I was shell shocked and fell on top of the ammo storage. At that moment another round penetrated the turret and killed the loader.[12]

---

11 See Drabkin, p. 66.
12 See Drabkin, p. 134.

T-34 COMMANDER'S VIEW

View through the PT-47 sight. Unlike the Panther, the T-34 did not have a gunner so there was no one to give commands to, the commander firing the gun himself.

View through the TMFD-7 sight as an AP round richochets off the Panther. Other than telling the driver to stop or the loader to load a shell there was little crew interaction.

Both Polyanovski and Bryukhov survived the battle but losses were heavy. In Polyanovski's battalion, only a single platoon of T-34s was left, and Bryukhov lost all three of his T-34s and ten of 12 crewmen in a matter of minutes. The more experienced Soviet tankers learned to take the springs out of their turret hatches, allowing them to escape more rapidly in the event of a hit. The Waffen SS Panthers had the tactical edge in this action because they were occupying hull-down positions and were supported by assault guns and 88mm flak guns. However, this tactical success did not prevent the fall of Kharkov. Operation *Rumantsyev* had cost the Soviet 1TA and 5GTA over 1,700 T-34 tanks but had decisively seized the initiative from von Manstein.

RETREAT TO THE DNEPR RIVER, SEPTEMBER 8–29

After the fall of Akhtyrka and Kharkov, the Soviets began their advance to the Dnepr River against fierce resistance from Army Group South. Soviet probing attacks often ran into German ambushes. Junior Lieutenant Polyanovski was given a new tank and crew for the pursuit phase:

> At dawn on 2 September, our three tanks were sent out to conduct a reconnaissance in force – that's the military term for it, but in reality to get killed. The Germans opened

T-34 ENGAGEMENT SEQUENCE

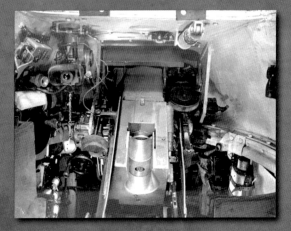

A T-34/76 platoon is on line in a defilade position in a dried-out stream gully, awaiting a German armor attack. The tanks all have BF-350A armor-piercing high explosive rounds loaded. The sergeant is scanning to his left with the rotating PT panoramic sight when the first rounds from a Panther land 80m to his right rear. He immediately scans to the right and spots a Panther 800m away and switches to the TMFD sight. The loader releases the main gun's safety and cradles an AP round in his arms.
The commander lays the cross hairs on the Panther and fires with his foot pedal. The round impacts in front of the Panther and throws up a splash of dirt. The loader instantly loads another AP round. The commander uses his hand elevation wheel to add 5 degrees and fires again. He sees a brief spark as his second round strikes the Panther's front slope and ricochets off. Having seen the ineffectiveness of his APDS rounds against the Panther's front slope, the commander decides to fall back to the next ravine and try to work around for a flank shot. As the T-34 traverses down into the

T-34/76 turret interior. The eyepiece for the PT-47 rotating periscope is toward upper left of this photo. The padded eyepiece for the TMFD sight is just to the left of the main breech gun, and next to the turret elevation handle.

streambed, the driver reports that both adjacent tanks from their platoon are burning.

fire and we fired back . . . I had to look into the periscope and bend toward the gun sight, and it was when I was looking through the sight that we got hit. The round pierced the turret above my head. It didn't hit me, but slivers of armor struck my head, tore my helmet and damaged my skull. I fell on the tarpaulin covering the ammo. After that a fire started, since the next thing to get hit was the engine compartment. Much later I found out that the loader's head was smashed . . . [13]

Polyanovski survived the destruction of his second T-34. However, the German panzer units were so depleted after seven weeks of continuous combat that von Manstein realized that he lacked the resources to stop the Soviet juggernaut. On September 8, von Manstein asked permission to withdraw his forces behind the Dnepr River, but Hitler refused. Although Das Reich's Panther battalion scored an impressive small rearguard victory near Kolomak against the Soviet 1st Mechanized Corps on September 12 and 13, Army Group Center was no longer capable of maintaining a continuous front. Hitler finally authorized a withdrawal on September 15, but it was nearly too late. On September 18, Stavka gave Vatutin the 3rd Guards Tank Army (3GTA) under Colonel-General Pavel Rybalko. Two days later, this mass of armor began a rapid advance toward the Dnepr. After marching over 160km in two days, Rybalko's 56th Guards Tank Brigade established a bridgehead over the Dnepr at Bukrin on September 22. The operational mobility of the T-34 prevented von Manstein from establishing an effective defense behind the Dnepr.

The retreat to the Dnepr was a disaster for the three Panther battalions in Grossdeutschland, SS-Das Reich, and the 11th Panzer Division (52nd Panzer Battalion was now redesignated as I/Panzer 15). Eighty Panthers were lost in September, mostly immobilized vehicles blown up to prevent capture. Grossdeutschland, with 18 Panthers and a few Tigers left, tried to establish a defensive position around Kremenchug but failed to prevent the 5GTA from gaining a crossing there on September 29.

A Panther Ausf. A command tank on the outskirts of a burning village. The Panther's thinner side armor was vulnerable if ambushed by Soviet antitank guns or T-34s lurking in such villages. (Author's collection)

13 See Drabkin, p. 68.

MELITOPOL, OCTOBER 2–24

After Army Group South began retreating to the Dnepr, Hitler briefly hoped that Army Group A's 6th Army might prevent the Soviet south and southwest fronts from reaching the lower Dnepr. Two of the new Panther battalions were directed toward this sector in the hope of preventing a Soviet breakthrough. A single company of Major Fritz Fechner's II/Panzer Regiment 23 arrived at Stalino on September 4, but quickly got itself surrounded and had to be rescued. The rest of the battalion was assigned to the 23rd Panzer Division but by then the 6th Army was in full retreat toward the Dnepr. Fechner was able to mount a counterattack against the 23rd Tank Corps near Pavlograd and inflict some losses, but by the end of the month his battalion was combat ineffective. Fechner's battalion had to blow up most of its disabled Panthers in the retreat to the Dnepr and only had three to six operational tanks for the rest of the year.

The German 6th Army established the Wotan Line around Melitopol, and on October 8, the I/Panzer Regiment 2 of the 13th Panzer Division arrived to provide a mobile reserve. However, before the battalion was fully assembled, the Soviet 20th Tank Corps and 4th Guards Mechanized Corps (4GMC) with over 200 T-34s launched a major attack against the Wotan Line. On October 10, part of I/Panzer 2 fought in the "tank battle of Oktoberfeld" in which the Soviet attack was repulsed with 30 percent losses. Melitopol finally fell on October 23, but Oberleutnant Graf Ledebur, commander of the 2nd Company, led a counterattack against the 4GMC at Kalinovka on October 24 that destroyed 35 T-34s. In the first two weeks in combat, the I/Panzer Regiment 2 had destroyed over 80 enemy tanks, but the constant road marches had incapacitated more than half the battalion due to mechanical breakdowns, and once the battalion had to retreat, most of the immobilized Panthers were blown up. Even the new Panther Ausf. A lacked the mechanical reliability to compete with the fast-moving T-34s in protracted mobile warfare.

OVERLEAF
Haupsturmführer Friedrich Holzer's SS Panther company ambushes the lead battalion of the Soviet 219th Tank Brigade around Kraschanitschen, northeast of Kolomak, September 12, 1943. This scene depicts the opening moment of the ambush, with a company-size force of Panther tanks engaging an attacking Soviet tank brigade, arrayed in two battalion wedges. Holzer was awarded the Knight's Cross for this action.

A Panther company massing for an attack. In order to avoid Soviet air and artillery attacks, the Panthers had to be dispersed and well camouflaged until the moment for action arrived. (Author's collection)

After fighting off the Soviet advance guard for several more days, the last Panthers crossed the Dnepr at Kherson, and the Germans blew up the bridges. Neither the II/Panzer 23 nor the I/Panzer Regiment I had seriously delayed or even hurt the Soviet advance to the Dnepr, and within a month of deployment, these battalions were reduced to ineffective remnants.

FASTOV, BRUSILOV, AND RADOMYSHL, NOVEMBER 15–DECEMBER 31

Despite desperate German counterattacks during October, Army Group South was unable to crush any of the Soviet bridgeheads over the Dnepr or to prevent the capture of Kiev by the 1st Tank Army on November 6. However, the Soviet armor spearheads were overextended after fanning out from Kiev, and von Manstein saw a chance to repeat his successful "backhand blow" formula. Von Manstein persuaded Hitler to give him all available armor reinforcements, and by November 9, he was able to mass six Panzer divisions in General Herman Balck's 48 Panzer Corps near Berdichev. Two new Panther units arrived for the counterattack: the I/Panzer Regiment 2 under Major Ernst Phillip and the SS-Leibstandarte's I/SS Panzer Regiment 1 under Sturmbannführer Herbert Kuhlmann. Combined, the Germans were able to mass 585 tanks for the counterattack, including about 70 Panthers and 30 Tigers. Von Manstein intended to attack into the left flank of Rybalko's 3rd Guards Tank Army (3GTA) near Fastov, encircle the Soviet armies on the west bank of the Dnepr, and recapture Kiev.

The German counteroffensive began in heavy rain on November 15. During the nine days of the counterattack, Kuhlmann's I/SS Panzer Regiment 1 destroyed about 40 enemy tanks but lost seven Panthers destroyed and 54 broken down or damaged.

A Panther conducting a movement to contact with infantry support. After *Zitadelle*, the lack of effective infantry, artillery, and air support greatly reduced the Panther's combat potential. (Robert L Hunt Library)

Phillip's I/Panzer Regiment 2 also destroyed about 40 tanks but lost six Panthers destroyed and about 30 out of action. The 7th Guards Tank Corps and part of the 9th Mechanized Corps suffered about 30 percent losses in the German counterattack, but the Leibstandarte had failed to capture Brusilov and the 3GTA was not encircled. The superiority of the KwK 42 gun on the Panther mattered little in this battle since most actions had been fought at ranges of 600–800m among wooded areas and small villages. The Panther units also found it increasingly difficult to come to grips with the T-34s without running through a gauntlet of 76mm and 85mm AT guns, hidden in the woods and villages. By this time, Soviet tank battalions had developed a tactic to fight Panthers and Tigers that, while costly, usually worked. Upon running into Panthers, a T-34 battalion would deploy two companies on line to fix the enemy while using the third company to flank the Germans. Having greater numbers and more mobile tanks allowed Soviet commanders to seize and retain the initiative in spite of better German gunnery.

Von Manstein's counterattack at Fastov pushed the 3GTA onto the tactical defensive, and the Germans wanted to renew the push before the Soviets could recover. On December 6, the 48th Panzer Corps attacked toward Radomyshl and succeeded in overrunning parts of the Soviet 60th Army, but the Germans lacked the strength to annihilate isolated units. Before the Germans could finish off the Soviet units around Radomyshl, a Soviet flanking move by the 25th Tank Corps at Meleni caused Balck to call off the attack. Leibstandarte and the 1st Panzer Division rapidly shifted to the west of Meleni and struck the 25th Tank Corps on December 19. In four days of tough fighting, the Soviets lost about 100 T-34s, but the two best German panzer divisions were reduced to only a few dozen tanks each, and the 48th Panzer Corps had

A Panther Ausf. D of SS Das Reich's 4th Panzer Company, I/SS Panzer 2 operating in the wooded terrain near Fastov during the German counterattack in November 1943. The T-34 could ambush the Panther in this type of terrain with a good chance of success. (Bundesarchiv BILD 1011-571-1721-13)

The ability of the T-34 to cross makeshift bridges and ford rivers frustrated German plans to use the Ukraine's river obstacles to stop the Soviet advance. (Courtesy of the Cental Museum of Armed Forces Moscow)

to shift to the defense on December 23. Von Manstein believed that these series of spoiling attacks had destroyed about 700 Soviet tanks in November to December and would prevent the Soviets from breaking out of the Kiev bridgehead. However, von Manstein once again seriously underestimated the Soviet ability to regenerate combat power. German intelligence had missed the transfer of large Soviet armor reinforcements into the Kiev area, giving Vatutin's 1st Ukrainian front a decisive advantage in numbers.

TANK AMBUSH

On September 12, 1943, the 219th Tank Brigade with about 60 T-34 tanks and part of the 19th Mechanized Brigade with about 25 tanks began to penetrate the German lines around Kraschanitschen. The T-34s advanced in v-shaped wedges easily overcoming the antitank trenches (1). The first wave of T-34s tanks destroyed the forward German positions and the infantry were forced to retreat (2). However, the Soviets did not notice

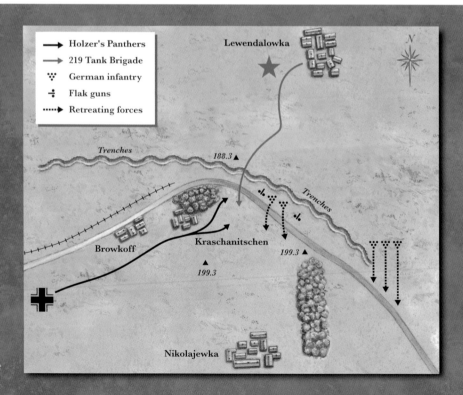

Holzer's Panthers
219 Tank Brigade
German infantry
Flak guns
Retreating forces

Lewendalowka

Trenches

188.3 ▲

Trenches

Browkoff

Kraschanitschen

199.3 ▲

▲ 199.3

Nikolajewka

Vatutin's offensive began on December 24 and quickly overran the German infantry units around Brusilov. Balck was outnumbered 5:1 in armor and could only mount a series of delaying actions to slow the Soviet advance. Between December 24 and 31, Vatutin lost almost 200 T-34s, although Zhitomir fell on December 31.

* * *

The tank battles west of Kiev in November to December 1943 were one of the last major German counteroffensives on the Eastern Front, and they were ultimately unsuccessful. Although the Germans claimed these actions and further small successes around Anamyenka were tactical victories, the fact is that they did not destroy any major Soviet units or delay Vatutin's breakout offensive. The Panther units achieved isolated successes, which German propaganda emphasized, but there were just too few tanks operational to make a real difference. Furthermore, they had failed to successfully perform the breakthrough role for which they had been created. Indeed, the Panther actually performed better in a defensive role, picking off T-34s advancing over open ground, but this role surrendered the initiative to the fast-moving T-34 armies. Additionally, the Soviets had finally learned to use combined arms tactics effectively by late 1943, and the integration of T-34s with supporting AT guns and motorized infantry was a combination that the Panthers could not defeat.

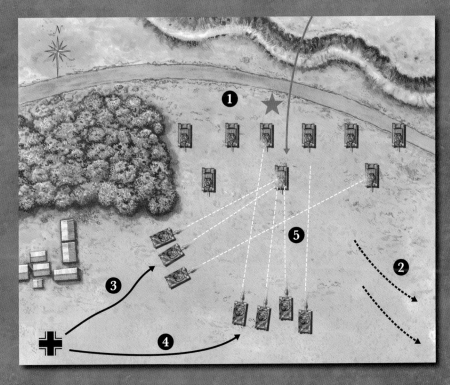

that a small group of Panther tanks from I/SS Panzer Regiment 2, commanded by Haupsturmfuhrer Friedrich Holzer, were approaching from the west and had just moved into hull-down ambush positions. Holzer split his outnumbered Kampfgruppe into two teams, one to hit the Soviets from the flanks (3) and one from the front (4). In around 40 minutes, the Panthers destroyed 28 T-34s in the "kill zone" without any losses (5).

STATISTICS AND ANALYSIS

PRODUCTION

A total of 842 Panther Ausf. D and 908 Panther Ausf. A models were built in 1943. From May to December, an average of just over 200 Panthers were built each month. However, only 1,071 Panther tanks, or 60 percent of those built, actually reached the Eastern Front in 1943. The balance remained in training units and new battalions that were being formed. Thus, despite the efforts lavished on developing and establishing a robust manufacturing base, the fielding of the Panther tank in 1943 failed to achieve the goals necessary to regain a degree of superiority.

In contrast to the German problems in fielding the Panther, Soviet industry was able to produce 15,812 T-34/76 tanks in 1943. Monthly production of the T-34/76 was about 1,300 machines. Production of the T-34 was aided by a mature design that had been simplified for mass production. Indeed, by mid-1943, the Germans were being outproduced by almost 3:1. Despite their technical merits, Tiger and Panther tanks constituted only 41 percent of German tank production in 1943, with the Pz IV remaining the backbone of panzer units. The commitment of so many industrial resources to an untried tank design at the expense of the proven Pz IV only served to starve the frontline units of effective tanks when they needed them most. It was this fear of disrupting production that caused the Soviet GKO to defer introducing a successor to the T-34/76 until absolutely necessary. The Soviet decision

ORDER OF BATTLE
Soviet Tank & Mechanized Corps in Ukraine 1943 that fought Panther units

CORPS	TANK UNITS	NUMBER OF T-34s	ASSIGNMENT	COMMANDER	ACTION
3rd Mechanized Corps	1 GTB 49 TB 14, 16, 17 TR	195	1TA	MGN Semen Krivoshein	Syrtsev/Dubrova
6th Tank Corps	22, 112, 200 TB	148	1TA	MGN Andrei Getman	Verkhopen'ye Tomarovka
	86 TB (Separate)	50	1TA	Colonel Agafonov	Verkhopen'ye
31st Tank Corps	100, 237, 242 TB	155	1TA	MGN Dmitri Chernienko	Verkhopen'ye Borisovka
5th Guards Tank Corps	20, 21, 22 GTB	150	6GA	MGN Andrei Kravchenko	Grayvoron
4th Guards Tank Corps	12, 13, 14 GTB	122	27A	MGN Pavel Poluboyarov	Achtyrka
1st Mechanized Corps	3, 4, 9 TR 219 TB	160	53A	MGN Mikhail Solomatin	Lyubotin Kolomak
5th Guards Mechanized Corps	51, 54, 55 GTR 24 GTB	160	5GTA	MGN Boris Skvortsov	Lyubotin
10th Tank Corps	178, 183, 186 TB	150	40A	MGN Vasilii Alekseev	Trostyanets
23rd Tank Corps	3, 39, 135 TB	150	3GA	MGN Efim Pushkin	Pavlograd
4th Guards Mechanized Corps	37, 38, 39 GTR 36 GTB	120	3GA	MGN Trofim Tanaschishin	Melitopol Kalinovka
20th Tank Corps	8GTB 80, 155 TB	171	61A	MG Ivan Lazarev	Melitopol
18th Tank Corps	110, 180, 181 TB	100	5GTA	MGN Boris Bakharov	Znamyenka
29th Tank Corps	25, 31, 32 TB	100	5GTA	MGN Ivan Kirichenko	Mishurin Rog Znamyenka
8th Mechanized Corps	116 TB 41, 83, 139 TR	100	5GTA	MGN Abram Khasin	Znamyenka
25th Tank Corps	111, 162, 175 TB	200	13A	MGN Fedor Anikushkin	Meleni
7th Guards Tank Corps	54, 55, 56 GTB	200	3GTA	MGN Kirill Suleikov	Fastov Brusilov
9th Mechanized Corps	47, 53, 74, 166 TR 59 GHTR	50	3GTA	MGN Konstantin Malygin	Brusilov

to defer upgrading the T-34 was costly to Soviet frontline tankers in the Ukraine in 1943, but it ensured that Soviet generals would have the numbers to conduct sustained high-intensity operations.

STRENGTH AT THE FRONT, UKRAINE, 1943

At the beginning of *Zitadelle*, Army Group South (AGS) had 91 Tigers and 200 Panthers (plus 1,010 Pz III and Pz IV tanks) opposing 3,600 T-34s. By December, AGS had only 54 operational Tigers and 80 Panthers (plus 350 Pz III/IV tanks) to hold off about 5,000 T-34s. Thus, despite the destruction of over 14,000 T-34s in 1943, German armor strength versus the Red Army fell in the last six months of 1943. The critical weakness of the Panther was its poor operational readiness (OR) rate due to persistent mechanical problems. Other than the first two days of *Zitadelle*, the Panther frontline operational strength was usually well below 100 tanks. In fact, it was not until April 1944 that the Germans again had at least 100 operational Panthers on the Eastern Front. Only one out of eight Panther battalions sent to the Eastern Front in 1943 managed to keep at least half its tanks operational for one week. The I/Panzer Regiment 1 had an OR rate of 57 percent after nine days at the front but dropped to

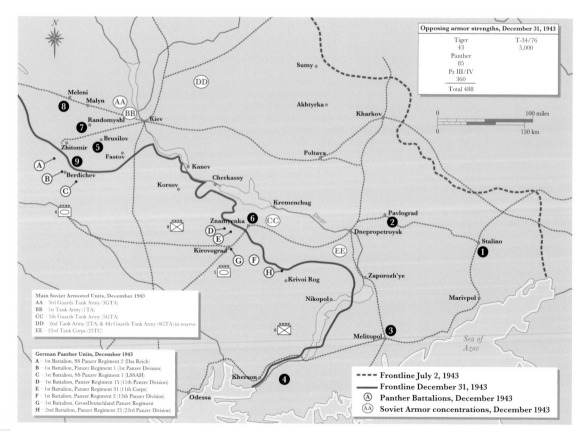

38 percent after three weeks. In contrast, most Pz IV battalions had around 65 percent readiness during the last half of 1943. While exact figures for T-34 readiness in specific units are unknown, overall numbers indicate that the T-34 usually had around a 90 percent OR rate before an offensive and about 50–70 percent during operations.

LOSSES

During 1943, the Red Army lost over 14,000 T-34/76 tanks, including about 6,000 lost fighting AGS from July to December 1943. During the last half of 1943, 493 Panthers were lost. Furthermore, over 50 percent of Panthers lost were destroyed by the Germans when forced to retreat. German crew losses in Panther units were not as severe as tank losses. The 51st Panzer Battalion suffered only 72 dead in July to August 1943, or slightly more than one death for each Panther destroyed. Soviet analysis indicated that 81 percent of hits on T-34s were on the hull and only 19 percent on the turret. Over half of all hits failed to penetrate the armor. During the fighting in July, 26 percent of T-34s destroyed were hit by 88mm guns, 40 percent were hit by 75mm guns, and 33 percent were hit by 50mm guns. Less than 1 percent of Soviet tanks knocked out by 75mm guns in 1943 were hit at ranges greater than 1,400m and less than 10 percent were hit beyond 1,000m. Roughly 60 percent of tank engagements occurred between 200–600m, and 10 percent were destroyed at 200m or less. Despite the supposed safety of diesel fuel, about 25 percent of T-34s that were hit caught fire. Soviet tank crew losses were extremely heavy, with only about 25–30 percent of tank crews surviving the destruction of their vehicles.

MAP KEY:
SEPTEMBER–DECEMBER 1943

1. September 4: One company of II/Panzer Regiment 23 arrives to bolster 6th Army defense around Stalino but is surrounded near Mospino by Soviet attack. The company is rescued by a 17th Panzer Division counterattack.
2. September 11–21: Remainder of II/Panzer Regiment 23 (23rd Panzer Division) arrives in 1st Panzer Army area and participates in counterattacks near Pavlograd against the Soviet 23rd Tank Corps.
3. October 9–10: I/Panzer Regiment 2 (13th Panzer Division) arrives near Melitopol on October 2, and helps to hold Wotan Line against Soviet 4th Guards Mechanized Corps and 11th Tank Corps. This is the first Panther unit at the front with mostly Ausf A models. On October 24, 2nd Company destroys 35 Soviet tanks near Kalinovka.
4. October 31: I/Panzer Regiment 2 participates in counterattack east of Kherson against Soviet 4th Guards Mechanized Corps that succeeds in preventing the 4th Mountain Division and Group Becker from being encircled and destroyed.
5. November 15–24: 1st Panzer Division and Leibstandarte SS Adolf Hitler (LSSAH), both moved in by rail for major counterattack by 48th Panzer Corps against Soviet 1st TA west of Kiev. Attack starts with about 65–70 operational Panthers and succeeds in defeating 5GTC and 8GTC at Brusilov.
6. December 5–8: I/Panzer Regiment 15 (11th Panzer Division) and I/Panzer Regiment 31 attempt to defeat 5GTA advance upon Znamyenka with about 30 Panthers. Panthers are able to destroy several dozen T-34s from 18th and 29th Tank Corps but cannot prevent fall of Znamyenka.
7. December 6–14: 1st Panzer and LSSAH continue attack toward Radomyshl and inflict another defeat on 1TA.
8. December 16–23: 1st Panzer and LSSAH attempt to encircle three Soviet tank corps (4GTC, 5 GTC, 25TC) in Meleni Pocket. The Germans inflict another defeat upon 1TA but are unable to close the pocket.
9. December 24–31: Soviet 1TA and 3GTA launch major winter offensive that rips open 4th Panzer Army front. 48th Panzer Corps, with about 45 operational Panthers, is unable to stop Soviet armor from seizing Zhitomir, although they are able to inflict heavy losses.

AFTERMATH

By the end of 1943, the German armored forces in the Ukraine were severely outnumbered by the Red Army. The introduction of the Panther tank had failed to reverse the situation. Indeed, the Panther was essentially an experimental design in 1943, and it was plagued with mechanical reliability problems long after its initial introduction at Kursk. Although the Ausf. D and A models were powerful gunnery platforms, the Panthers were so mechanically fragile that they could rarely move far from railheads, and more were lost from noncombat reasons than from action against Soviet units. The introduction of the Panther Ausf. G in March 1944 did resolve some of the more nagging problems, such as engine fires and weak final drives, but the Panther remained an expensive fuel hog and which became increasingly vulnerable to Soviet 85mm and 122mm tank guns by mid-1944.

Despite a major effort to mass produce the Panther, the quantity of operational Panthers available in frontline armor units was fewer than 100 for most of 1943. The Wehrmacht was unable to convert the Panther's theoretical potential into a real battlefield advantage in 1943. While on occasion, the small Kampfgruppes of Panthers bloodied the Soviet T-34 tank brigades in the Ukraine in 1943, these were tactical successes that did not translate into any real change in the Wehrmacht's deteriorating operational situation. The total number of T-34s knocked out or destroyed by Panthers in July to December 1943 was probably in the vicinity of 500, or about 8 to 10 percent of the total number lost in the Ukraine in that period. On the other hand, T-34s destroyed relatively few Panthers in 1943 – probably no more than several dozen – but they kept them on the run, which led to breakdowns. In spite of the Panther's advantage in firepower, the T-34's mobility and reliability advantages were more germane to actual battlefield necessities in the Ukraine in 1943, allowing the Red Army to gain and hold the initiative by maneuvering large tank formations across hundreds of kilometers of steppe.

In contrast the Red Army had fixated on a quantitative approach to tank warfare. It was not until mid-1943 that the Soviets realized that their heretofore qualitative advantages in tank warfare had disappeared as new German designs were introduced, and the decision to up-gun the T-34 to an 85mm gun was made rather slowly and production began in March 1944. Despite the shortcomings of the basic T-34/76 design by late 1943, Koshkin had provided the Red Army with a tank that could move hundreds of kilometers on its own tracks without breaking down, which could ford rivers or cross them on pontoon bridges, and which could operate for months with minimal maintenance. In designing the Panther, the Germans ignored many of the T-34's best qualities and bet their fortunes on an overly complicated and ultimately flawed design.

ORDER OF BATTLE
German Panther battalions in Ukraine in 1943

PANZER BATTALION	NUMBER OF PANTHERS ASSIGNED	DATE ARRIVED AT FRONT	ASSIGNMENTS	COMMANDER(S)
Pz. Battalion 51	96	July 1, 1943	Grossdeutschland PzGr. Division	Hauptmann Heinrich Meyer (Jan. 13–Aug. 19, 1943) **KIA**. Major Julius Pfeffer Sept. 15–20 Nov. 1943)
Pz. Battalion 52	96	July 4, 1943	Grossdeutschland PzGr. Division	Major Gerhard Tebbe (July 5–6, 1943). Hauptmann Georg Baumunk (July, 6–24, 1943). Major Karl von Sivers (July 22, 1943–March 1944)
I/SS Pz - 2	71	August 22, 1943	SS Das Reich PzGr. Division	SS-Haupsturmführer Hans Weiss
I/Pz. - 15 (redesignated Pz. Bn. 52)	96	August 24, 1943	11th Panzer Division	Major Karl von Sivers (July 22, 1943–March 1944)
II/Pz - 23	96	August 31, 1943	23rd Panzer Division	Major Fritz Fechner
I/Pz. - 2	71	October 2, 1943	13th Panzer Division	Hauptmann Bollert (Oct. 2–21, 1943) **KIA**. Hauptmann Georg Grüner (Oct. 22, 1943–Mar. 11, 1944)
I/SS Pz - 1	96	November 9, 1943	SS Leibstandarte Panzer Division	SS-Sturmbannführer Herbert Kuhlmann
I/Pz. - 1	76	November 11, 1943	1st Panzer Division	Major Ernst Phillip
I/Pz. - 31	76	December 5, 1943	XI Corps (15 Dec 43) 3rd Panzer Corps (27 Dec 43)	Major Hubertus Feldtkeller

BIBLIOGRAPHY

Bessonov, Evgeni, *Tank Rider: Into the Reich with the Red Army*, Casemate, Philadelphia, 2003.

"Description of Sighting Equipment for 76 mm Tank Gun in Russian T-34 Tank," translated by School of Tank Technology, September 1943.

Drabkin, Artem, and Oleg Sheremet, *T-34 in Action*, Pen & Sword, Barnsley, UK, 2006.

Fey, Will, *Armor Battles of the Waffen SS, 1943-45*, Stackpole Books, Mechanicsburg, PA, 1990.

Gätzschmann, Kurt, *Panzerabteilung 51 Heeresgruppe II/Panzerregiment 33 1943–1945* (unpublished manuscript).

Glantz, David M., *Forgotten Battles of the German-Soviet War, Vol. V The Summer–Fall Campaign, 1 July – 31 December 1943*, self-published, 2000.

Glantz, David M., and Jonathan M. House, *The Battle of Kursk*, University of Kansas Press, Lawrence, KS, 1999.

Hughes, Dr. Matthew, and Dr. Chris Mann, *The T-34 Russian Battle Tank*, MBI Publishing Co., Osceola, WI, 1999.

Jentz, Thomas L., *Germany's Panther Tank: The Quest for Combat Supremacy*, Schiffer Military History, Atglen, PA, 1995.

Jentz, Thomas L., *Panzertruppen: 1943–1945*, Schiffer Military History, Atglen, PA, 1996.

Jung, Hans-Joachim, *The History of Panzer Regiment Grossdeutschland*, J. J. Fedorowicz Publishing, Winnipeg, Canada, 2000.

Kolomyjec, Maksym, and Janusz Ledwoch, *Panthers and Tigers in the Kursk Bulge 1943*, Wydawnictwo Militaria, Warsaw, 2004.

Lehmann, Rudolf, *The Leibstandarte III*, J. J. Fedorowicz Publishing, Winnipeg, Canada, 1990.

Lodieu, Didier, "Le Bataillon de Panther de la 9.Pz.Div." in *Russie ou l'historique de la Pz.Abt. 51* (2e partie), *39/45 Magazine*, No. 187, February (2002).

_____ "La Panther-Abteilung de la 9. Pz.-Div. ou la II./Panzer-Regiment 33 puis la Panzer Abteilung 51 Historique du Pz.-Rgt.33, " *39/45 Magazine*, No. 169, July (2000).

Rahn, Walter, "Fighting Withdrawal of Kampfgruppe von Sivers as 'Floating Bubble' in the Vorskla Valley from Tomarovka via Borissovka-Grayvoron-Pirasevka-Kirovka as far as Achtyrka in August 1943," unpublished paper by former orderly officer of Panzer Battalion 52.

Schneider, Wolfgang, *Panzer Tactics: German Small-Unit Armor Tactics in World War II*, Stackpole Books, Mechanicsburg, PA, 2005.

Sewell, Stephen, "Why Three Tanks?" *ARMOR*, July–August 1998.

Sharp, Charles C., *German Panzer Tactics in World War II*, published by George F. Nafziger, West Chester, OH, 1998.

_____, *Red Storm: Soviet Mechanized Corps and Guards Armored Units, 1942 to 1945*, George F. Nafziger, West Chester, OH, 1995.

_____, *School of Battle: Soviet Tank Corps and Tank Brigades, January 1942 to 1945*, George F. Nafziger, West Chester, OH, 1995.

_____, *Soviet Armor Tactics in World War II*, George F. Nafziger, West Chester, OH, 1999

Trojca, Waldemar, "Sd. Kfz. 171 Pz.Kpfw. V Panther," *Model Hobby*, Katowice, Poland, 2003.

The German Tank Platoon in WWII: Its Training and Employment in Battle, George F. Nafziger, West Chester, OH, 2002.

Vuksic, Velimir, *SS Armor on the Eastern Front 1943–1945*, Fedorowicz Publishing Inc., Winnipeg, Canada, 2005.

Zaloga, Stephen J., "Soviet Tank Operations in the Spanish Civil War," *Journal of Slavic Military Studies* Vol. 12 No. 3.

Zetterling, Niklas, *Kursk 1943, A Statistical Analysis*, Frank Cass, London, 2000.

Russia Battlefield website: www.battlefield.ru

INDEX

References to illustrations are shown in **bold**.